# AMERICAN COMPASSION IN INDIA: GOVERNMENT OBSTACLES

## HEARING

BEFORE THE

# COMMITTEE ON FOREIGN AFFAIRS HOUSE OF REPRESENTATIVES

ONE HUNDRED FOURTEENTH CONGRESS

SECOND SESSION

DECEMBER 6, 2016

## Serial No. 114–241

Printed for the use of the Committee on Foreign Affairs

Available via the World Wide Web: http://www.foreignaffairs.house.gov/ or
http://www.gpo.gov/fdsys/

U.S. GOVERNMENT PUBLISHING OFFICE

22–864PDF                    WASHINGTON : 2017

For sale by the Superintendent of Documents, U.S. Government Publishing Office
Internet: bookstore.gpo.gov    Phone: toll free (866) 512–1800; DC area (202) 512–1800
Fax: (202) 512–2104    Mail: Stop IDCC, Washington, DC 20402–0001

## COMMITTEE ON FOREIGN AFFAIRS

EDWARD R. ROYCE, California, *Chairman*

CHRISTOPHER H. SMITH, New Jersey
ILEANA ROS-LEHTINEN, Florida
DANA ROHRABACHER, California
STEVE CHABOT, Ohio
JOE WILSON, South Carolina
MICHAEL T. McCAUL, Texas
TED POE, Texas
MATT SALMON, Arizona
DARRELL E. ISSA, California
TOM MARINO, Pennsylvania
JEFF DUNCAN, South Carolina
MO BROOKS, Alabama
PAUL COOK, California
RANDY K. WEBER SR., Texas
SCOTT PERRY, Pennsylvania
RON DeSANTIS, Florida
MARK MEADOWS, North Carolina
TED S. YOHO, Florida
CURT CLAWSON, Florida
SCOTT DesJARLAIS, Tennessee
REID J. RIBBLE, Wisconsin
DAVID A. TROTT, Michigan
LEE M. ZELDIN, New York
DANIEL DONOVAN, New York

ELIOT L. ENGEL, New York
BRAD SHERMAN, California
GREGORY W. MEEKS, New York
ALBIO SIRES, New Jersey
GERALD E. CONNOLLY, Virginia
THEODORE E. DEUTCH, Florida
BRIAN HIGGINS, New York
KAREN BASS, California
WILLIAM KEATING, Massachusetts
DAVID CICILLINE, Rhode Island
ALAN GRAYSON, Florida
AMI BERA, California
ALAN S. LOWENTHAL, California
GRACE MENG, New York
LOIS FRANKEL, Florida
TULSI GABBARD, Hawaii
JOAQUIN CASTRO, Texas
ROBIN L. KELLY, Illinois
BRENDAN F. BOYLE, Pennsylvania

AMY PORTER, *Chief of Staff*    THOMAS SHEEHY, *Staff Director*
JASON STEINBAUM, *Democratic Staff Director*

# CONTENTS

# AMERICAN COMPASSION IN INDIA: GOVERNMENT OBSTACLES

---

## TUESDAY, DECEMBER 6, 2016

House of Representatives,
Committee on Foreign Affairs,
*Washington, DC.*

The committee met, pursuant to notice, at 10:09 a.m. in room 2172, Rayburn House Office Building, Hon. Edward Royce (chairman of the committee) presiding.

Chairman ROYCE. This hearing will come to order.

And to put this hearing in perspective, I want to make a point about India. As chairman and as a leader of the India Caucus, I helped build that caucus from just 12 members to 160 members. I managed the U.S.-Indian civil nuclear agreement on the House floor and beat back the anti-India amendments, which would have killed the agreement.

I carried the original bill to lift sanctions on India in the 1990s and traveled with President Clinton on his historic trip to India. I was tasked with briefing President Bush on the importance of deepening our relationship with India on counterterrorism and on trade. And I flew into Bhuj with USAID the day after the Gujarat earthquakes and first met then Chief Minister Narendra Modi, who was on the ground bringing order out of chaos. I admired him for the work he had done, and I admire him today for what he is trying to do in India.

I traveled to Mumbai the day after the terrorist attacks to meet with Indian intelligence officials and press the Government of Pakistan to either try the LeT terrorists or turn them over to The Hague to be tried for crimes against humanity by the International Criminal Court. I was one of the leading voices pushing for a U.S. visa for Chief Minister Modi. I extended the invitation for Prime Minister Modi to address a joint meeting of Congress, a historic occasion we celebrated this June, and I also personally hosted the Prime Minister at a reception in his honor.

My chief of staff, Amy, and her daughter, who is Indian American, have for years sponsored and built a relationship with a girl in India. These two 7-year-olds draw and send pictures to each other. They share what games they like to play and what food they like to eat. That bonding experience is the same for the other American families that also send, each of them, $38 every month to 145,000 children, the poorest of the poor in India. These are children who would otherwise be without enough food and without the fees that they need for their education.

Americans have been sending these checks, through an organization called Compassion, to India for nearly 50 years. In India, it is the single largest contributor of aid for children living in extreme poverty.

Now, Amy and thousands of other American families are being obstructed from supporting these children. This is despite the best effort of Secretary of State John Kerry and of myself and others on the committee. We have spent 9 months and hundreds of hours dealing with the Indian bureaucracy on this, and it looks like the bureaucracy is trying to run out the clock.

We as Americans deal with American bureaucracy. It is part of the job here as members of the House of Representatives. We work for our constituents, but we don't always win. Bureaucracies are stubborn, stubborn things in America, let me tell you.

Presidents can have a vision, but that vision can be frustrated by the bureaucracy. Prime Minister Modi has a vision about India. He is self-made. He was never a member of some elite. He was the son of a poor man. As he says, "the son of a poor man standing in front of you today," and as he said, "I am devoted to the development of all; the Dalit, the oppressed, the underprivileged, the deprived. A government is one that thinks and hears the voice of the people. A government must be for the poor."

But bureaucracies have their own dynamics, and they can stifle any President or Prime Minister's dreams. For the past 9 months this committee has had meetings, written letters, made  phone calls, and for that I thank our members.

This isn't a hearing that the committee expected to be holding. It is my hope that by bringing attention to this issue, as we are doing here today, the 145,000 children will not be tragically denied the services they desperately need and that American families like Amy's can continue to send the $38 a month for food and education fees to the poorest of the poor.

I know the ranking member will be with us momentarily. In the meantime, I will introduce our panel, and then move to the ranking member's remarks once he arrives.

This morning, we are pleased to be joined by a distinguished panel. Mr. Stephen Oakley is the general counsel and vice president of the General Counsel's Office at Compassion International. He joined Compassion in 2011 where he is responsible for overseeing their domestic and international legal and government affairs.

Mr. John Sifton is acting deputy Washington director and Asia advisory director at Human Rights Watch. He began working at Human Rights Watch in 2001 where he has focused on Afghanistan, Pakistan, and India, and previously he worked for the International Rescue Committee.

Dr. Irfan Nooruddin is a professor of Indian politics and director of the India Initiative at Georgetown University. He is the author of Coalition Politics and Economic Development Credibility and the Strength of Weak Governments.

Without objection, by the way, the witnesses' full prepared statements will be made part of the record. Members are going to have 5 calendar days to submit statements or questions or extraneous material for the record.

I am going to go to our ranking member, Mr. Eliot Engel of New York. But I am going to ask, when we go to the panelists, if you will summarize your testimony to 5 minutes, and then we will go to questions.

Mr. Eliot Engel of New York.

Mr. ENGEL. Thank you, Mr. Chairman. Thank you for calling this hearing today. I welcome the chance to speak with you about Compassion International's recent struggles in India, and I know this is an issue close to your heart.

As you know, I share your concern about challenges some NGOs are facing in India. My staff and I tried to assist in resolving the situation, and I hope following this hearing we can find a way forward on this issue. And I am grateful, as always, for your leadership.

To our witnesses, welcome to the Foreign Affairs Committee. We are grateful for your time and expertise.

More than 20 years ago, I was one of a handful of Members of Congress who founded the caucus on India and Indian Americans. At that time the U.S. relationship with India focused more on what our two countries couldn't do together rather than what we could do together. Today, in my view, the U.S. relationship with India is one of our most important, driven by our shared interests and shared values.

We have made progress in so many areas. India now participates in more military exercises with the United States than any country in the world. Once the sticking point between our governments, nuclear cooperation has become the lynchpin of a renewed U.S.-India partnership.

On climate change, India has already ratified the Paris Agreement. Trade between India and the United States continues to expand. Supporting thousands of American jobs, it has nearly tripled from 36 billion in 2005 to over 107 billion in 2015. India's strategy to expand economic engagement in Asia aligns closely with our own Asia rebalance.u

The list goes on and on from space exploration, to shared concerns in the Indian Ocean region, to economic growth; we are collaborating on more issues than ever before. Much of this progress is due to our people-to-people ties rooted in the 3 million strong Indian-American community. Thanks to their advocacy and the hard work of dedicated leaders of all political ideologies in both countries, the United States and India are now closer than ever before. But this doesn't mean that the United States and India will agree on everything. And when we don't see eye to eye, we need to have honest discussions and work toward good solutions. And that is why we are doing this hearing today on the NGOs and other things involving the U.S.-India relationship.

I discussed earlier the importance of the values that the United States and India both share. This goes beyond the cliche of being the world's oldest and largest democracies, we embrace our traditions of political freedoms, of free and fair elections and of a vibrant, vocal civil society.

The United States nor India, neither one of us, are strangers to contentious political debate. Our recent elections are a great example of that, and India has a long rich tradition of raucous political campaigns. The free debate is the cornerstone of democracy. So I was concerned by reports earlier this year that a college student, a student body president, was arrested for making what was deemed antinational statements. College campuses have long been a hotbed of political activism. And whether we find this activity agreeable or objectionable, these democracies need to protect the right of free expression and free assembly, and again I know the chairman is very concerned about that as well.

I have been concerned by reports that NGOs are having difficulty registering and operating in India. Civil society plays a pivotal role in democracy, holding government accountable and standing up for the rights of marginalized groups. So it is troubling that a country with such a long tradition of an empowered and active civil society might be going down this path. We can't avoid the hard questions or avoid discussions simply because they are difficult conversations to have. This is how democracies work, warts and all.

So I look forward to hearing from our witnesses today about all of these issues, the tremendous progress and potential of the U.S.-India relationship, but also in areas like international child abduction, where there is still a lot of work to be done. If we stay committed to deepening this venture further, if we think long term while working to meet day-to-day challenges, then this relationship will help both our countries become stronger and more prosperous and will become one of the defining partnerships of the 21st century.

Thank you, and I look forward to your testimony.

Thank you, Mr. Chairman.

Chairman ROYCE. Thank you, Mr. Engel.

We go now to Mr. Oakley.

## STATEMENT OF MR. STEPHEN OAKLEY, GENERAL COUNSEL AND VICE PRESIDENT OF THE GENERAL COUNSEL OFFICE, COMPASSION INTERNATIONAL

Mr. OAKLEY. Good morning, Mr. Chairman, Ranking Member Engel, members of the Foreign——

Chairman ROYCE. Mr. Oakley, there is a button right there that you can press. We can hear you there.

Mr. OAKLEY. Thank you, Mr. Chairman.

Good morning, Mr. Chairman, Ranking Member Engel, members of the Foreign Affairs Committee. My name is Stephen Oakley. I am Compassion International's general counsel. It is my privilege to speak with you today on the topic of Compassion's specific experience in India and the reason that Compassion is merely weeks away from permanently withdrawing its operations in India.

By way of a brief background, since 1952, it has been the mission of Compassion to help children living in extreme poverty around the world. And today, Compassion is the world's largest child sponsorship NGO with 1.9 million children in 26 countries in Asia, Africa, and Latin America.

Compassion has been in India since 1968, and for five decades now, Compassion has worked without incident under the authority of successive Indian Governments. That abruptly changed in 2013 when Compassion encountered the first of a series of legal and regulatory attacks. This came about in the form of tax cases, in which the government assessed over $18 million in corporate income tax on the charitable donations to our locally incorporated South India entity.

That was followed by a series of different attacks. Intelligence bureau investigations, enforcement directorate cases, you have before you as an exhibit to my brief a copy of the Ministry of Home Affairs order. It is a prior approval order that prevents Compassion from getting any money into India without the advanced clearance of the ministry, which we have found to be a fiction.

Finally, both of the FCRAs of Compassion's locally incorporated entities have been denied. We have sought legal advice from multiple lawyers, chartered accountants in India. And to a person, they have assured us and provided us the advice that our operations are legal and lawful under the laws of India. And to a person, they have suggested that to the extent the law is being broken in India, it is being broken by the Indian Government in advancing extremely aggressive and legally unsupported interpretations of existing law, knowing that charities often lack the resources or expertise to challenge these interpretations, and when they do, the challenges will take years in court.

In discussions with other faith-based NGOs and my own reading of the relevant portions of the Indian constitution and their Tax Act and their FCRA laws, I have come to the conclusion that Compassion is experiencing an unprecedented, highly coordinated, deliberate, and systematic attack to drive Compassion out of India. Anecdotally, I am hearing similar stories from other faith-based and civil society organizations.

The reason, apparently, is the Government of India wrongly believes that faith-based organizations are using humanitarian efforts to convert Indians to Christianity. And these attacks are occurring under the guise of regulatory compliance. But these reasons are a fiction. It is religious discrimination, pure and simple.

The behavior of the Indian Government toward Compassion and other faith-based NGOs is in my view illegal. It is inconsistent with the values of freedom of expression and freedom of religion, which the Indian constitution specifically guarantees.

Now, as a committee, why should you care? First, as one of the largest NGOs in the world and as the number-one importer of foreign NGO currency into India, if Compassion is forced to withdraw, in my view, this represents a green light to the Indian Government to take the same or similar action against a range of other faith-based and secular NGOs. That is a real risk.

Second, if the rule of law is breaking down in India, as I believe it is, that impacts not only civil society organizations, not only the NGO sector. That presents a real risk to foreign business in India, to United States businesses in India. The rule of law is essential for all corporations, including not-for-profits and for-profits.

Finally, you should care because the Indian Government has made no plan, no provision whatsoever, for the 145,000 children that Compassion cares for in India. There is no plan for them when we depart.

To that end, I have three requests. First, we humbly ask that this committee demand that the Indian Government immediately rescind the prior approval order, which our counsel tell us was illegally issued and is illegal under their law.

Second, we ask that this committee demand that the Indian Government reinstate the FCRAs of both of Compassion's locally incorporated field offices in India that have operated for over a decade successfully. Our counsel tells us their revocation was illegal.

Third, we ask that you continue to make the fair treatment of NGOs in India a precondition across a spectrum of other issues between India and the United States. Link it to other issues that India cares about. Consequences only have value if they result in changed behavior, so I ask that you send the Indian Government a strong message that this matters to the United States.

Again, there is no plan for these children if we depart. So we ask you to ask the Indian Government to reconsider its decision. Thank you very much. I would be happy to take your questions.

[The prepared statement of Mr. Oakley follows:]

Statement before the

House Committee on Foreign Affairs

*Compassion International Operations in India*

Presented by Stephen Oakley

Senior Vice President and General Counsel, Compassion International

Tuesday, December 6, 2016

Chairman Royce, Ranking Member Engel, and distinguished members of the committee, it is an honor to appear here today.

My name is Stephen Oakley. I lead our General Counsel Office at the faith-based non-profit, Compassion International, which is headquartered in Colorado Springs, Colorado. I come to you today to discuss challenges we are facing with our operations in India. But first, let me share a little about our ministry.

Compassion International is the world's leading authority in holistic child development of children living in extreme poverty. Holistic child development means we take a long-term approach to poverty alleviation, going beyond simple assistance in the lives of the children and families we serve. We begin, in some cases, with prenatal care, then continue our program through the duration of childhood, and offer leadership development opportunities for young adults. The impact of our program extends far beyond basic relief efforts to transform lives and communities.

Compassion began its work with children in post-war Korea in 1952. Today, Compassion operates in 26 countries in Asia, Africa and Latin America and Caribbean, providing a range of services designed to meet the physical, mental, emotional and spiritual needs of impoverished and at-risk children. Compassion's support includes many different types of interventions, such as nutrition, health care, counseling, education and job training. As a faith-based non-governmental organization (NGO), Compassion believes that poverty is not just physical or economic, but that it impacts every aspect of a child's life, including spiritual poverty. Poverty tells a recurring lie that poor children don't matter. Therefore, we believe combatting child poverty requires a holistic approach that encompasses every aspect of a child's life.

### Why Compassion Works with Churches

Compassion's delivery model is unique among NGOs — Compassion works exclusively with local Christian churches who are best equipped to understand and meet the unique needs of children in their communities. The primary reason we have chosen this model is that the moral and spiritual values which the world-wide church embodies are consistent with those of Compassion and its donors. A second reason we have chosen this model is the NGO community's familiar problem of the "last mile." Getting humanitarian services to the last mile — the point of delivery in extremely poor contexts — is difficult and costly. Compassion has solved this challenge by working with local churches and utilizing them as the delivery system. This approach has benefits for both parties and it allows Compassion to work in very difficult and impoverished contexts efficiently, while also building up the local church as a center of community, safety and hope. This approach has proven incredibly effective. Compassion now works in partnership with over 7,000 churches worldwide, benefiting 1.9 million children supported by a one-to-one child sponsorship model.

### Compassion in India

Compassion opened operations in India in 1968. For 48 years Compassion has operated continuously and lawfully, helping over a quarter of a million children break the cycle of poverty. Until 2016, Compassion sent nearly $50 million per year in humanitarian aid to India, funding nearly 145,000 sponsored children in some of Indian's most impoverished and remote regions. Compassion's church partners in India employ hundreds of staff through more than 580 child development centers staffed entirely by Indians. Compassion only works through churches which possess a valid license to receive foreign aid.

### Religious Discrimination Disguised as Taxation

India's Ministry of Home Affairs (MHA) regulates foreign aid through the Foreign Contribution Regulation Act (FCRA). In 2011, MHA revised the purpose of FCRA to:

> "Regulate the acceptance and utilization of foreign contribution or foreign hospitality by certain individuals or associations or companies <u>and to prohibit acceptance and utilization of foreign contribution or foreign hospitality for any activities detrimental to the national interest</u> and for matters connected therewith or incidental thereto." (Emphasis added).

At the time of the revision, the significance of this language was not fully understood by many NGOs. The law does not define which activities are "detrimental to the national interest." However, MHA has used this language as their basis to target religious charities that express views or engage in activity which is lawful, but contrary the current government's ideology. The result has been a clear chilling effect on the free-expression of religion across India.

In 2011, Compassion's field-partner in South India, Caruna Bal Vikas (CBV), was notified that it was selected for an audit by the Commissioner of Income Tax (CIT). In May of 2013, after reviewing the thousands of pages of documents provided by CBV, the CIT asserted that CBV had violated its purposes as a charitable public trust by transferring funds to Indian charities that are registered as religious. Ultimately, the CIT assessed CBV more than $18 million in illegal tax. This tax was on charitable funds contributed by donors in the United States and twelve other countries intended to help Indian children living in extreme poverty. In making its demand, the CIT ignored that it has no legal mandate to inquire, let alone determine, whether a charity's activities are charitable or religious. The CIT's illegal tax theory is intended to harass, intimidate and ultimately drive out Compassion and its partners from India.

9

Compassion sought the advice of six different legal and tax counsels in India, all of whom concluded that the CIT had no legal basis for the tax assessment. Compassion is confident its partners and Compassion have followed Indian tax law. Despite the clear inapplicability of the law and lack of authority of the CIT to examine CBV's corporate purposes, the CIT seized CBV's bank account, forcing them to cease operations in May of 2014. CBV's legal challenges to these tax assessments remain pending in court.

### The Home Ministry's Attack on Freedom of Religion

Article 25 of the Indian Constitution, entitled "Right to Freedom of Religion" provides: "Subject to public order, morality and health and to the other provisions of this Part, all persons are equally entitled to freedom of conscience and the right freely to profess, practise [*sic*] and propagate religion." Article 15 provides: "The State shall not discriminate against any citizen on grounds only of religion, race, caste, sex, place of birth or any of them." (Emphasis added). Article 14, entitled "Right to Equality" provides: "The State shall not deny to any person equality before the law or the equal protection of the laws within the territory of India."

MHA has repeatedly disregarded these constitutional protections. In May of 2016, MHA placed Compassion on a list of international NGOs that had to seek prior clearance from MHA before transferring funds to Indian charities that serve Indian citizens. What was the offense? Compassion's charity towards India's poorest children is rooted in Christian values. MHA evidently views Christian values as a threat to the national interest, particularly if those values are taught to the poor. MHA has never provided Compassion or its partners with any explanation for the prior clearance order, nor has it ever responded to Compassion's multiple efforts to engage in dialogue. This includes Secretary of State Kerry's appeal to Foreign Minister Sushma Swaraj requesting MHA reconsider its baseless decision.

In August of 2016, harassment of Compassion extended to its Compassion East India (CEI) operations, this time in the form of an Enforcement Directorate investigation into "anti-national activity," again without any evidence, or opportunity to be heard. Despite CEI's full cooperation, that investigation remains pending.

Finally, in November of 2016, Compassion learned that both its partners, CBV and CEI, had been denied FCRA renewal without explanation. These decisions are being appealed, but as MHA well knows, any legal challenge to these decisions will take years. MHA knows that, in the case of Compassion and all other charities that they have targeted, time is to their benefit.

### MHA's Pattern of Harassment

Over the last three years, the Commissioner of Income Tax (CIT) and the Intelligence Bureau have each made multiple visits to CBV, CEI and dozens of their local church partners in India. In two instances, they have commenced "interviews" after 5 p.m. and interrogated Indian staff overnight — in one instance for eleven hours. They intimidate and ask leading questions like: "you are converting children to Christianity, aren't you?" Even if those false accusations were true, the government is harassing Indian citizens engaged in lawful conduct. Computers and records have been confiscated, more than ten visa applications have been denied in the last two years and in one case, (the author's) an existing visa was cancelled with no explanation. Most recently, MHA has prevented the return of $330,000 dollars in aid that Compassion attempted to transfer to its Indian partners. The money cannot be received by the intended partner in India or returned to Compassion. This low-level harassment and intimidation by MHA is widespread and not limited to Compassion.

### India's Violation of Indian Law

While India's government has wrongly accused Compassion of engaging in illegal conversions and anti-national activity, it has simultaneously ignored and violated its own laws. Compassion's counsel in India has advised that the Reserve Bank of India (RBI) prior clearance notice misinterprets and directly violates the FCRA in the following ways.

1. First, Section 11(3)(iv) of the FCRA provides when a foreign agency can be placed under a prior permission category. The section states that foreign aid sources can be placed on a prior permission category only after notification is placed in India's Official Gazette explaining who shall obtain prior permission, and the sources of foreign aid which shall be accepted with prior permission from the Central Government, among other requirements. Compassion was given no such notice.

2. Second, the prior clearance notice states that the RBI was directed by MHA under Section 46 of the FCRA. The RBI does not have any authority to enforce the FCRA. Specifically, Section 46 does not provide discretionary power to India's Central Government; it only empowers it to direct or seek aid from other authorities in executing the Act. Therefore, an order under Section 46 must be supported by another provision of the Act. This order specifies no such authority.

3. Third, Section 9(d) restricts how a foreign aid recipient may be placed under the prior clearance category. MHA may require a registered organization to seek prior clearance before receiving foreign aid from a foreign source – but not a blanket prohibition against a single foreign organization or a particular foreign source of aid, as is the case here.

4. Fourth, Section 9(d) may apply only if the government has reason to believe that accepting aid will result in hampering public interest, religious harmony, etc. Such orders are against the aid recipient in India; therefore, they cannot be made without first formally communicating the order to the recipient and providing an opportunity for the recipient to be heard. According to a recent Delhi High Court case, if an order is not passed under the requirements of Section 9(d), is it void.

5. Finally, the burden is on MHA to establish specific findings of an FCRA violation before issuing any prior permission order. MHA has never even notified Compassion that it believes a violation occurred.

In summary, the FCRA registration renewals for Compassion's partners were rejected in violation of the law. The only reason for denying the renewal was *"On the basis of Field Agency Report, the competent authority has decided to refuse your application for renewal."* The Field Report was never shared with Compassion or its partners; therefore, it cannot be the basis for an alleged FCRA violation. In fact, there was never an inquiry or proceeding pending under the FCRA or a show cause order for any possible violation. The FCRA permits a registration denial only when an organization has violated a provision of the FCRA. The registration rejection was simply ordered without proper application of the facts and the law.

MHA knows that they can use the inefficiency and massive delays of the Indian bureaucracy as a weapon – forcing charities like Compassion to either accept their determinations, or spend years seeking redress in a painfully slow and often corrupt legal system. In short, India's Home Ministry is using those aspects of India's bureaucracy, which are most in need of urgent reform, to systematically target NGOs with agendas and views that differ from its own.

### The Future of Compassion and other NGOs in India

The present-day reality in India is sobering. India has a population of 1.3 billion people in a land area slightly more than one-third the size of the United States. The United Nations estimates that over 30 percent of the world's 400 million children living in extreme poverty are in India alone. India has nearly one million registered charities and is one of the world's largest recipient of NGO aid. Despite this reality, India's present government appears to be on a campaign to eliminate foreign NGOs — particularly those that the government perceives have agendas which are not in alignment with its policies. In the past two years, the government has waged a quiet campaign against a range of charities, religious and non-religious, which the government perceives as a threat. This list includes Greenpeace, Ford Foundation, Amnesty International and a variety of others, large and small.

This is troubling for a country which prides itself on the label of "the world's largest democracy." Indeed, the democratic ideal of freedom of religion and the free expression of religion, which are cornerstones of the Indian constitution, appear to be under attack from within India. This, combined with a culture of indifference to the poor, have led India to the brink of becoming a limited access country from the standpoint of the NGO sector, while simultaneously making no provision for the resulting burden that India will face on its own. While the government of India may not notice the expulsion of NGOs, India's 120 million children living in extreme poverty certainly will.

The United States is one of India's most important partners. In turn, India is a valued strategic partner of the United States. India remains a country that the U.S. should vigorously engage in a robust bilateral dialogue. This dialogue should include making the discriminatory treatment of NGOs a point of significant discussion in the broader U.S./India relationship. U.S. policy should include incentivizing India to protect freedom of all speech, protection of minority religions and perspectives, and care for the poor.

Using the Indian government's own numbers, just 4 percent of Compassion's funds in India are used for moral and spiritual values education – values which transcend all religions. The remaining 96 percent is the routine but essential provision of food, medicine, clothing, school fees and related humanitarian aid to support tens of thousands of at-risk infants, children and youth living in extreme poverty. Simply put, Compassion's primary mission is to release children from poverty, not convert them.

The measure of a constitutional democracy is not how it panders to the majority, but rather how it protects the minority. India is a wonderfully diverse country with dozens of ancient people groups, languages, cultures and religions. The present Indian administration needs to demonstrate that its weakest and smallest citizenry are afforded the same rights and protections and those in power.

To conclude, Compassion International is approximately three weeks away from permanently withdrawing its humanitarian operations from India. As the single largest contributor of aid for children living in extreme poverty in India, that is not our desire. Our hope is that this committee will act. Specifically, we ask that this committee demand that the government of India rescind the prior clearance order of MHA so that Compassion can fund the sponsored children under its care. Additionally, we ask this committee to demand that the government of India reinstate the FCRAs of Compassion East India and Caruna Bal Vikas, so that Compassion may pay its employees in India. Finally, on behalf of Compassion's 145,000 sponsored children and the remaining 130 million that other NGOs of all faiths attempt to serve, we ask that you use your influence as lawmakers to advocate for those that the Indian government ignores.

Chairman ROYCE. Thank you, Mr. Oakley.

We go to Mr. Sifton.

## STATEMENT OF MR. JOHN SIFTON, ACTING DEPUTY WASHINGTON DIRECTOR, ASIA ADVOCACY DIRECTOR, HUMAN RIGHTS WATCH

Mr. SIFTON. Thank you for providing me the opportunity to testify today. It may be a moment of transition here in Washington, but this hearing is actually extremely well-timed. As my copanelist has already noted, there is a troubling new crackdown underway in India today, especially in the last few months.

A large number of nongovernmental organizations—international, domestic, religious, secular—have faced increasing government harassment in the last few months and in the last few years, including intrusive and politically motivated legal scrutiny. And the U.S. Government, a close ally, needs to better respond. And the incoming Congress and incoming administration needs to give this issue more attention than it has already received.

My testimony, in summary, is about how the Indian Government is specifically creating for NGOs these problems. So let's go down to specifics.

The main and most powerful tool the Indian Government has for harassing NGOs is the Foreign Contribution Regulation Act, the FCRA. It is an overbroad and poorly worded, poorly drafted law that contains provisions that basically can be abused to block foreign funding for groups, deregister them, and stymie their activities.

The problems with the FCRA are twofold. First, it is overly intrusive. It basically gives the government too much power. The Home Ministry is given powers that it ought not to have, powers to look into an organization's specific projects and question them. Its provisions are both overbroad and overreaching. It gives the government the power to cut funding for organizations on the vague grounds that they are ''likely to affect prejudicially the economic interest of the State'' or its ''public interest.''

The FCRA has been used and abused by successive Indian Governments. The Congress government abused this law as well, but its use and abuse has increased significantly with the current BJP government. Last year the government used FCRA provisions to harass numerous NGOs, including Greenpeace India, as well as an organization run by the activist, Teesa Setalvad that has brought legal cases seeking justice for victims of the 2002 Gujarat violence. As you know, Prime Minister Modi was the chief minister in Gujarat in 2002, and there are numerous allegations about his complicity in the violence. So you can imagine that when people who are seeking justice for that violence are gone after, it very clearly looks politically motivated.

This May, the government suspended for apparently politically motivated reasons the FCRA's status of the Lawyers Collective founded by the prominent lawyers Anand Grover and Indira Jaising. The Lawyers Collective has represented Setalvad and the Greenpeace activists, who are targeted, among others. And just a few weeks ago, the government canceled the Lawyers Collective's registration under the FCRA.

Abuse of FCRA has intensified in recent months. In October alone, the government refused to renew the FCRA of at least 25 NGOs without valid reasons, lead us to issue a statement about it. Several domestic human rights groups were deregistered. The Ministry of Home Affairs told media that the NGOs were denied FCRA registration because their activities were ''not in the national interest.''

Several of the specific cases from October are outlined in the written version of my testimony. But let me give the context. All of these new harassments under the FCRA come as attacks on freedom of expression and association in India have been on the rise. In the last 2 years, Human Rights Watch has observed how Indian authorities have increasingly used the country's sedition law against peaceful critics, including activists and artists and students, for alleged ''antinational'' speech.

Other overbroad and vaguely worded laws, including India's criminal defamation and hate speech laws, are also used to harass and prosecute those who have expressed dissenting or unpopular or minority views.

The harassment of NGOs is taking place in a context in which religious minority groups, in particular Muslims and Christians, are at increased risk. Let's be clear, since the BJP came into power in 2014, militant Hindu groups have been increasingly threatening and sometimes even physically assaulted Christians and Muslims.

The consequences of these tensions go beyond human rights concerns, as my copanelists have mentioned, and affect even India's economy. So I think it is important that the U.S. Government and incoming administration take this seriously not just from a human rights point of view but from an economics of view.

The basic recommendation my testimony gives are that, first, the incoming administration and the incoming Congress and Members should raise concerns about the FCRA more publicly. When U.S. officials speak with Indian officials, they be should raise concerns about the FCRA directly and mention publicly that they are doing so.

They should enlist the support of U.S. corporations and other private sector actors whose charitable activities are impacted by this. I think if U.S. corporate and business leaders are also raising this, it will have an enormous impact beyond, you know, groups like Human Rights Watch raising these issues.

And last, just speak out about the rise in violent attacks by Hindu nationalists on Christians and Muslims and other minority groups. I mean, the Government of India needs to hear complaints from outside the country about these issues.

The written version of my testimony outlines those recommendations in more detail, but thank you for allowing me to testify today. And I will be glad to answer questions.

[The prepared statement of Mr. Sifton follows:]

## US Congress – House Foreign Affairs Committee
## Hearing on Harassment of Non-Governmental Organizations in India
## December 6, 2016

### Testimony of John Sifton
### Asia Policy Director
### Human Rights Watch

Thank you for providing me the opportunity to testify today. It may be a moment of transition here in Washington, but this hearing is extremely well timed.

A troubling new crackdown on civil society is underway in India, especially in the last few months. A large number of non-governmental organizations (NGOs) have faced increasing governmental harassment including intrusive and politically motivated legal scrutiny, and the US government—a close ally—needs to respond. The incoming Congress and administration need to give this issue more attention in the coming year.

Let me start by outlining how the government is creating trouble for NGOs that question or criticize the government or its policies.

The most powerful tool for Indian government harassment of NGOs is the Foreign Contribution Regulation Act (FCRA), an overbroad and poorly drafted law that contains provisions that can be used to block foreign funding for groups and stymie their activities. First, the FCRA is overly intrusive: it makes regulation a matter under the jurisdiction of the Home Ministry instead of being vested with authorities responsible for compliance with tax laws; other provisions give authorities too much power to scrutinize organizations' specific programming on a project-by-project basis. Second, its provisions are both overbroad and overreaching: the law gives the government the power to cut funding to organizations with programming or projects on vague grounds that they are "likely to affect prejudicially. . . the economic interest of the State" or its "public interest."

The FCRA has been used and abused by successive Indian governments. But its use has increased significantly in the current Bharatiya Janata Party (BJP) government. Last year, the government used FCRA provisions to harass several NGOs, including Greenpeace India, as well as an organization, run by activist Teesta Setalvad, that had brought legal cases seeking justice for victims of the 2002 communal violence in Gujarat. As you know, Prime Minister Narendra Modi was then the chief minister there, and there are numerous allegations about his complicity in the violence.

This May, the government suspended for apparently politically motivated reasons the FCRA status of the Lawyers Collective, founded by prominent lawyers Anand Grover and Indira

Jaising, that has represented Setalvad and a Greenpeace activist, among others. In November, the government canceled the group's registration under FCRA.

Abuse of FCRA has intensified in recent months. In October the government refused to renew the FCRA of at least 25 NGOs without valid reasons, including several human rights groups. The media quoted Ministry of Home Affairs officials as saying that the NGOs were denied permission under the FCRA because their activities were not in the "national interest." India's National Human Rights Commission has questioned the recent decisions and said that, "[p]rima-facie it appears FCRA license non-renewal is neither legal nor objective and thereby impinging on the rights of the human rights defenders both in access to funding including foreign funding."

One of these groups is the Centre for Promotion of Social Concerns, a prominent Indian human rights organization better known by its program unit People's Watch. The only reason the government offered in denying its FCRA renewal was that its decision was based "on the basis of field agency report." Civil society leaders generally assume this refers to reports of intelligence agencies or law enforcement personnel.

Similarly, the Indian NGO Hazards Centre, a unit of the Sanchal Foundation working on community and labor rights programming, was also told that its FCRA renewal application was denied "on the basis of field agency report." In October the FCRA renewal for the Indian Social Action Forum (INSAF), a network of NGOs and people's movements, was also denied.

People's Watch, for their part, challenged the government's decision in court; a government lawyer told the court that the decision was taken in the "public interest," but argued that the government was exempt from giving specific reasons.

Indian rights advocates as well as Human Rights Watch have long argued that the FCRA's provisions are incompatible with India's constitution and international legal obligations. India's courts have generally ruled against the government when NGOs have contested the use of FCRA to cut their funding.

In April, the United Nations special rapporteur on peaceful assembly and association, Maina Kiai, issued a report analyzing the FCRA that concluded that the law's restrictions and rules "are not in conformity with international law, principles and standards."

NGOs' problems with the FCRA come as attacks generally on freedom of expression and association in India have been on the rise. Indian authorities have increasingly used the country's sedition law against peaceful critics including activists, artists, and students for alleged "anti-national" speech. Other overbroad and vaguely worded laws, including India's criminal defamation and hate speech laws, are used to harass and prosecute those expressing dissenting, unpopular, or minority views.

In several cases, when interest groups claiming to be offended by books, movies, or works of art pushed for censorship or harassed the authors, the government has allowed them a "heckler's veto" rather than protecting those under attack.

This harassment of NGOs is taking place in a context in which religious minority groups, in particular Muslim and Christians, are at increased risk. Since the BJP came to power in 2014, militant Hindu groups have increasingly threatened and sometimes physically assaulted Christians and Muslims. Several BJP leaders have made inflammatory remarks against minorities. Prime Minister Modi has spoken out at times against attacks and inflammatory remarks, but too little and too rarely, and local authorities typically fail to properly investigate or prosecute persons responsible for attacks.

The consequences of these tensions go beyond human rights concerns and affect the totality of India's situation—even its economy. Economists and business leaders have warned that India's stability and economy are at risk if Modi fails to control Hindu extremism and the growing restrictions on freedom of expression.

In 2015, Moody's Analytics warned that Modi risked losing domestic and global credibility if he didn't rein in the more extremist members of his administration who had engaged in "belligerent provocations" of India's religious minorities.

Human Rights Watch makes the following recommendations to members of Congress, and urges this committee to work with the incoming administration to act on them.

The US government should:

- Raise concerns about the FCRA more publicly. When US officials speak with Prime Minster Modi, they should raise concerns about the FCRA directly and mention publicly that they did so. US officials should also urge Modi to end government harassment of NGOs, while encouraging him to ask parliament to amend the FCRA to only regulate corruption and deprive the Home Ministry authority to block funding for NGOs. Existing legislation applicable to both the private and non-profit sector, [such as the Unlawful Activities (Prevention) Act 1967 and the Prevention of Money Laundering Act,] are far more effective in dealing with issues like terrorism financing and money laundering.

- Enlist the support of US corporations and other private sector actors in India whose charitable activities are impacted by the FCRA to raise concerns with relevant Indian government officials that cracking down on funding of NGOs is inconsistent with the Modi government's focus on opening India to foreign investment.

- Speak out about the rise in violent attacks by Hindu nationalists on Christians, Muslims and other minority groups.

Thank you for allowing me to testify today and I would be glad to answer any questions you may have.

---

Chairman ROYCE. Dr. Nooruddin.

## STATEMENT OF IRFAN NOORUDDIN, PH.D., HAMAD BIN KHALIFA PROFESSOR OF INDIAN POLITICS, WALSH SCHOOL OF FOREIGN SERVICE, GEORGETOWN UNIVERSITY

Mr. NOORUDDIN. Good morning, Chairman Royce, Ranking Member Engel, members of this distinguished committee, committee staff. It is a pleasure to be here this morning and to have this opportunity to speak to you.

The FCRA, or the Foreign Contributions Regulatory Act of 2010, which is at the core of today's hearing, is a revision and amendment of an earlier act that was passed in 1976. The FCRA of 1976 was passed in the height of India's Emergency period, which is the one brief interlude where India veered toward an autocratic rule before coming back to its democratic core. I would say that over the 40 years since the FCRA 1976 was passed, the India-U.S. relationship has deepened and has become a truly strategic partnership thanks in no small part to the efforts of many of you.

But the FCRA hasn't improved with time. And, in fact, its anti-democratic roots are very much on display, as has been remarked upon by our copanelists today. While I talk about FCRA in civil society, I do think, though, it is important to put into context the broadest strategic relationship that has been built, thanks to the investments of the United States Government across administrations and by the Indian Government across its governments. The defense relationship is stronger and deeper, with more potential than at any prior time in either country's history.

The signing of the LEMOA agreement earlier, the start of the joint exercises in Malabar, the defense procurement potential between India and the United States all represent opportunities that even 10 years ago, at the height of that civil nuclear deal that Chairman Royce referenced, would have been quite unthinkable to have happened so quickly. So this is a really tremendous success.

In energy and the environment, there is a level of dialogue between the United States Government and the Indian Government that I think transcends just energy and environment and has business implications for technology transfer and technical assistance that is quite far reaching and transformative. And the fact that between September of this year, when the Indian Government stated a position on the Paris Agreement that it could not imagine signing it, to today, 2 months later where it has, is really a revelation that United States pressure on issues of climate change and energy paid dividends.

The Indian Government recognizes the United States as a crucial partner, and I think sees its viewpoints as those that have to be taken seriously. This is all enhanced by a very vibrant commercial relationship that is in its own way developed by that diaspora population that has now become a prominent part of American society, contributing to every aspect of American life.

So it is against a very promising and optimistic background that we come here today to discuss what has remained a sore point, and that is India's record on civil society and on its base core democratic principles. This is especially troubling given that the two countries are united not just by strategic interests but by a shared commitment to principles of democracy and to religious freedom.

India is among the most religiously diverse countries in the world. With one of the largest populations of Muslims, a Christian population that dates back millennia, and is home to major world religious. And so any strikes against religious freedom in India should trouble us all, not just those who are particularly interested in India. If religious freedom cannot succeed in India, it has a very poor chance of succeeding in other parts of the developing world.

So what happened? From my perspective, it is important to understand that the FCRA in 1976 was passed so that the Indian Government could regulate foreign contributions to pro-democracy, antigovernment organizations but in the context of an autocratic government of Prime Minister Indira Gandhi, who was very afraid of domestic dissent, pushing back against the Emergency.

This has continued and all governments have used the FCRA to stifle NGOs. The question, therefore, today is sort of how bad has it gotten and what are the implications for religious freedom?

My colleagues have mentioned a couple of numbers. The one I would point to you is that in 2012 there were 43,000 associations registered under the FCRA. Today, that number is halved. It is down to about 20,000. That is about 20,000 NGOs that either have chosen not to reapply for their licenses, or who have had their licenses not renewed by the Indian Government.

If you go to the FCRA Web site on the Ministry of Home Affairs, they list 11,300-plus NGOs that have not had their FCRA licenses renewed.

There are a number of reasons for this. Many of these are undoubtedly in violation of the letter of FCRA regulations. But the broader issue here is the transparency or lack thereof of the Indian Government and how it has enforced and how it has changed its interpretation of FCRA regulations over the last 4 years has placed a lot of NGOs in violation of a law that they thought they understood and thought that they were following. This has a chilling effect on civil society that has to be considered.

So just to close, and I am happy to take questions, I think the key recommendation I would make from my perspective is that the United States Government has to put pressure on the Indian Government to clarify and make transparent how it understands and plans to enforce the FCRA, what are the procedures for due process and for appeal for an association found in violation of the FCRA, and to assure all parties, both in India and in the United States, that it is not being used to target faith-based religious organizations that, I should make explicit, are not in violation of the FCRA simply by being faith-based or religious organizations.

There is nothing in the FCRA that prevents a faith-based organization from doing charitable work in India. I think we can come back to this in Q&A, but I think my colleagues have talked about the possibility of this being religious discrimination smuggled behind the guise of taxation. I am not sure that I would endorse that position fully. That requires deeper analysis, but I think there is enough to warrant real concern. Thank you.

[The prepared statement of Mr. Nooruddin follows:]

**House Foreign Affairs Committee Full Committee Hearing on
Indian Government Obstacles to Compassion International**

Prepared Testimony of Irfan Nooruddin

Hamad bin Khalifa Professor of Indian Politics and Faculty Chair,
Walsh School of Foreign Service at Georgetown University

Director, Georgetown University India Initiative

House Committee on Foreign Affairs

December 6, 2016

Irfan Nooruddin is the Hamad bin Khalifa al Thani Professor of Indian Politics in the Walsh School of Foreign Service at Georgetown University where he presently serves as Faculty Chair. He is the Founding Director of the Georgetown University India Initiative. He is the author of the new book *Elections in Hard Times: Building Stronger Democracies in the 21st Century*. His first book was *Coalition Politics and Economic Development: Credibility and the Strength of Weak Governments*. He has been a Fellow at the Woodrow Wilson International Center for Scholars.

Professor Nooruddin is on the editorial management team of *Studies in Indian Politics* and serves on the editorial boards of the *American Journal of Political Science, Comparative Political Studies, Georgetown Journal of Asian Affairs, International Studies Quarterly, International Studies Review,* and *Political Science Research & Methods*. He is a member of the Evidence in Governance and Politics network. Professor Nooruddin received his B.A. from Ohio Wesleyan University and his M.A. and Ph.D. from the University of Michigan.

The Georgetown University India Initiative builds on Georgetown University's core strengths—academic excellence, location in Washington, D.C., and Jesuit mission of service to the world—to advance research and teaching around India and world affairs and create a platform for high-level dialogue among American and Indian leaders from government, business, civil society, and the academy. More information is available at http://india.georgetown.edu.

Chairman Royce, Ranking Member Engel, members of the distinguished committee, and committee staff, thank you for the opportunity to testify today.

The U.S.-India partnership has continued to evolve under recent U.S. administrations, and the relationship has strengthened across multiple fronts, including defense collaboration, energy cooperation, and commercial ties. In addition, the Indian diaspora community in the United States makes up a vibrant political and economic constituency. While the strengthening of this strategic relationship is beneficial for the United States as we seek to foster global stability and free markets, India stands to reap significant benefits of this partnership. Therefore, the United States maintains strong leverage to engage India on the issue of NGO crackdown and foreign exchange management by their government. The current "prior permission" status of Compassion International in India is not an isolated event but it does not necessarily signify Indian governmental retaliation against faith-based – specifically Christian evangelical – organizations. Rather, this incident is consistent with a broader trend affecting many NGOs and nonprofits in India which are increasingly complaining of heavy-handed government regulation in what has led many social observers to raise alarms about an attack on civil society by the current government. Such alarmism is not entirely misguided but it is overblown. In enforcing the regulations of the Foreign Contribution (Regulation) Act (FCRA), the Government of India is acting fully within its rights as a sovereign state, and the reality is that a great many of the organizations that have lost their licenses since May 2014 were in violation of FCRA regulations. But it is also arguably true that many have violated the letter rather than the spirit of the law, and that the enforcement has been too often opaque and without clear explanation of cause. Further, while concerns that the Government of India has targeted faith-based Christian organizations disproportionately cannot be confirmed without more systematic analysis, anecdotal evidence does suggest that such concerns are not without warrant.

The critical point is that these incidents, troubling and unfortunate as they might be for specific institutions and their erstwhile beneficiaries, are but one part of the broader US-India relationship that has the potential for being a vital strategic partnership for the United States in the 21$^{st}$ Century. Investments in deepening this relationship have enjoyed bipartisan support in Congress and span administrations, and this commitment in turn affords the United States leverage in asking the Indian government to make the enforcement of its policies more transparent and to protect freedoms of association and speech for all civil society organizations without fear of interference.

## An Overview of the U.S.-India Strategic Partnership

The U.S.-India partnership has made great gains across defense, energy, and commercial cooperation in recent decades, and initiatives aimed at strengthening this relationship across these three metrics have received bipartisan support. A fuller accounting of the gains in various dimensions of the relationship are beyond the scope of my testimony today, but a good recent summary is provided by Assistant Secretary's Nisha Biswal's testimony to the Senate Foreign Relations Committee on May 24$^{th}$, 2016[1] and in the August 31$^{st}$, 2016, joint statement following the second Strategic and

---

[1] Available at http://www.foreign.senate.gov/hearings/us_india-relations-balancing-progress-and-managing-expectations-052416.

Commercial Dialogue.[2] Here I provide a précis of the key advances in the relationship over the past decade to set the context for my recommendations of how best to deal with the issues underpinning today's hearing.

In 2006, Congress passed legislation enabling a U.S.-India civil-nuclear deal that would allow the U.S. to export nuclear materials and equipment to India, so long as India signed the Treaty on the Non-Proliferation of Nuclear Weapons (NPT). This initiative was spearheaded by President George W. Bush, who viewed the agreement as an integral part of his non-proliferation strategy.[3] President Obama continued the trend of defense cooperation with India. After nearly a decade of talks, U.S. Defense Secretary Ash Carter and Indian Defense Minister Manohar Parrikar signed the Logistics Exchange Memorandum of Agreement (LEMOA) in 2016. LEMOA built and institutionalized foundational agreements to promote interoperability between the two militaries by creating a set of common standards and systems.

The United States and India have also strengthened ties related to energy cooperation. In 2009, the U.S. and India launched the Partnership to Advance Clean Energy (PACE), which works to accelerate inclusive, low-carbon opportunities for growth by supporting research and adoption of renewable energy technologies. The U.S.-India Energy Dialogue is held annually in order to track the progress of PACE and other levels of bilateral initiatives on energy cooperation.[4]

In October 2016, India ratified the Paris Climate Agreement, the world's first comprehensive climate agreement that aims to cut CO2 and greenhouse gas emissions. Under the terms of this agreement, India has committed to ensuring that 40% or more of its electricity will be generated by non-fossil sources by 2030. This was a bold commitment on behalf of India, the world's third-largest greenhouse gas emitter. In September 2016, India's representative at the G20 summit claimed that various legal impediments would make it impossible for the country to ratify the agreement. However, Indian officials changed their mind, partly due to strong U.S. pressure to sign on to the agreement. President Obama and Chinese President Xi Jinping made a public appearance in Hangzhou after ratifying the agreement, where President Obama remarked that the two countries were "leading by example." As the world's two largest economies and largest $CO^2$ and greenhouse gas emitters, their entrance into the agreement not only signaled strong international buy-in, but also put significant pressure on India to join the major political and economic powers in ratifying the agreement. That the pressure succeeded is credible evidence of India's desire to demonstrate that it should be considered a global leader in governance issues.

Commercial ties between our two countries have never been stronger. While there is a long ways to go, trade between India and the United States continues to grow in spite of a challenging global economic climate. U.S. investors continue to find opportunities in India and, encouragingly, Indian investors are looking to the United States to grow their businesses, generating jobs and prosperity. The Indian government has proven very receptive to feedback provided by U.S. businesses

[2] Available at http://www.state.gov/r/pa/prs/ps/2016/08/261405.htm.
[3] Kate Heinzelman, "Towards Common Interests and Responsibilities: The U.S.-India Civil Nuclear Deal and the International Nonproliferation Regime," in *Yale Journal of International Law*, Volume 33, Number 1 (2008), 448.
[4] U.S.-India Energy Cooperation, *U.S. Department of Energy*, 2016, http://energy.gov/ia/initiatives/us-india-energy-cooperation

and continues to streamline the investment process and to cut the redtape that had bedeviled previous efforts to make India's economy attractive to foreign investors. To be sure, much remains to be done to realize India's full potential as an investment destination, but the high levels of human capital and favorable demographic profile ensure that the economic relationship will continue to flourish for years to come. Of particular interest is the growing venture capital role played by Indian investors for start-up innovation in the United States; successful partnerships in this sector could lead to synergies in a variety of 21$^{st}$ century technology-leading domains. The uncertain future of the Trans-Pacific Partnership (TPP) makes the stronger economic relationship with India all the more important.

A final dimension on which I'd like to comment briefly is the affinity of values between the two nations. As the two largest democracies in the world, both India and the United States have long seen themselves as sharing a commitment to basic principles of human freedom and as beacons for other countries seeking to follow their examples. This affinity is enhanced by the vibrant and successful Indian diaspora population in the United States. At just about 3 million people, the Indian diaspora is the third-largest immigrant population in the United States. It is a young population with above-average education rates and income profiles, and it has become rapidly more politically organized and visible. President-elect Trump has named Indian-American Governor Nikki Haley as his pick to be the U.S. Ambassador to the United Nations, and the 2016 elections will send the first Indian-American to the U.S. Senate and four elected to this House of Representatives, including Rep. Ami Bera who serves on this committee. Given the tremendous pull of American higher education to talented Indian students, this population will likely continue to grow with great upside for the U.S. economy.

This brief overview confirms what we already know: India is a rising world power that should be a strategic partner of the United States. This partnership is enabled and strengthened by shared interests for the future of Asian and global governance, as well as a bedrock of common values and democratic principles. Yet, for all this optimism, there exist points of difference that need to be dealt with forthrightly as befits a strong relationship between friends. The issue being discussed today is one such point of contention that threatens to undermine the hard work of both sides in building a well-institutionalized partnership that spans administrations. I turn to this set of issues below.

## Compassion International

Compassion International (CI) is a child-advocacy ministry that pairs impoverished children in the developing world with sponsors online. Sponsors pay a small donation each month to sponsor a child. In turn, CI uses these funds to provide educational support, vocational training, leadership skills workshops, and spiritual and character development through its partner churches and denominations. CI invests at least of 80% of all funds raised by sponsorships and donations into their front-line ministry. The remaining funds are directed towards funding overhead costs, such as fundraising efforts and administrative support. In FY 2016, 82.4% of CI funds were directed to programs that directly benefitted children, and the remaining 17.6% supported overhead costs. Compassion International is rated highly by charity watchdog agencies in terms of financial health, accountability, and transparency. Charity Navigator gives it a rating of 84.45/100 on financial health, 100/100 on accountability and transparency, and an overall rating of 89/100.[5] CharityWatch gave the organization an "A" rating in 2016.[6]

Compassion International operates in 26 countries, and has had a presence in India since 1968. In order to maintain such high capacity, CI partners with affiliate agencies in-country to deliver services and support. Compassion International funds its affiliates in India, such as Caruna Bal Vikas, Chennai and Compassion East India, Kolkata. These affiliates also distribute funds to other NGOs. According to the CI website, some 145,000 Indian children participate in 570 child development centers in India. According to the Indian government, in 2011-12, CI was the single-largest foreign donor under FCRA.[7]

NGOs in India that receive foreign funds must be registered under The Foreign Contribution (Regulation) Act (FCRA). This act, enacted by Parliament in 2010 to replace the FCRA act of 1976, was established to regulate and monitor foreign contribution or hospitality to safeguard against "any activities detrimental to the national interest."[8] The main change in 2010 was to end the practice of permanent registration; henceforth, NGOs receiving foreign funds could receive a five-year FCRA licence that had to be renewed. While FCRA-registered, NGOs are allowed to receive foreign funding as long as they adhere to the regulations outlined in the FCRA, which mandates monthly reporting, along with several other accountability mechanisms, in order to foster transparency.[9] Of particular relevance here is the requirement that all organizations to which foreign funds might be disbursed need to be registered under FCRA.

According to the Ministry of Home Affairs (MHA), which monitors all foreign-funded nonprofits, Compassion International affiliate Caruna Bal Vikas (a registered FCRA-NGO) was distributing funds to nonprofits that were not registered with the FCRA, a violation of Section 7 of the FCRA. Under these terms, non-registered nonprofits do not have approval to receive donations from foreign organizations.[10]

On March 28, 2016 the MHA revoked Compassion International's FCRA registration, and placed the nonprofit on a "prior permission" list, an oversight mechanism that requires all donations to Indian NGOs to be pre-approved by the MHA. This prevents CI from transferring funds directly to its affiliate NGOs in India, which has severely limited its capacity. CI's Indian affiliates cannot receive any funds directly from the organization without MHA approval on a case-by-case basis. At a hearing of the Senate Foreign Relations Committee in May 2016, Colorado Senator Cory Gardner

---

[5] Charity Navigator is an independent U.S. charity watchdog organization that evaluates non-profits according to two metrics: financial health and accountability/transparency. "Compassion International," *Charity Navigator*, 2016, https://www.charitynavigator.org/index.cfm?bay=search.summary&orgid=3555.

[6] CharityWatch is an independent charity watchdog organization. "Compassion International," *CharityWatch*, 2016, https://www.charitywatch.org/ratings-and-metrics/compassion-international/172.

[7] https://fcraonline.nic.in/home/PDF_Doc/annual/ar2011-12.pdf

[8] See Foreign Contribution (Regulation) Act, 2010, https://fcraonline.nic.in/home/PDF_Doc/FC-RegulationAct-2010-C.pdf

[9] See Foreign Contribution (Regulation) Act, 2010, Section 17, https://fcraonline.nic.in/home/PDF_Doc/FC-RegulationAct-2010-C.pdf

[10] Rahul Tripathy, "US-based NGO, Compassion International, put on government watch list," *The Economic Times*, July 1, 2016.

voiced his concerns about the Indian government's treatment of Compassion International, calling the apparent crackdown "an attack on civil society."[11] In the same committee hearing, Assistant Secretary of State for South and Central Asia Nisha Desai Biswal emphasized that while the United States has a critical role to play in sharing experiences and best practices, the issue of religious freedom and religious tolerance is one that the Indian people, and their civil society, must grapple with. However, she also added that U.S. diplomats have raised concerns with their counterparts in India about "the regulatory and legal framework that seeks to constrain the activities of civil society organizations, whether they be Indian or international organizations."[12]

U.S. Secretary of State John Kerry voiced his concerns over the treatment of Compassion International in September 2016 during the strategic and commercial dialogue, and urged the MHA to reconsider its decision to put CI on the "prior permission" list.[13] MHA later approved, under the terms of "prior permission" Compassion International's fund transfers to 10 NGOs. An MHA official stated that CI sought permission to fund 250 NGOs during the fiscal year, all of which were Christian organizations. According to the ministry, some of these NGOs were found to be using funds to convert people to Christianity.[14] However, according to the FCRA Article 12, Subsection 14, there is no restriction on funding religious agencies unless they have been prosecuted or convicted for indulging in activities aimed at conversion through inducement or force, either directly or indirectly, from one religious faith to another.[15]

## FCRA and Civil Society in India

Compassion International is not alone. Growing constraints on NGOs and civil society organizations is an ongoing concern in India, and this practice is not confined to religious organizations. Several other high-profile foreign-backed NGOs have faced similar restrictions. There are currently 21 organizations backed by foreign donors that are under the government scanner and are placed on the "prior permission" list, mandating that any incoming donations to an Indian bank account be cleared with the Ministry of Home Affairs before reaching their accounts. Eight similarly-funded organizations were put under this level of scrutiny under the Congress Party, and 13 have been put under "prior permission" under the current government. According to the 2011-12 Annual Report of the MHA, in 2012 there were 43,000 organizations with FCRA registrations. Today, four years later, that number is halved, the result of non-renewals and the decision by many NGOs not to apply for renewal.[16] As of 22nd November 2016, the MHA lists 11,500 NGOs whose FCRA licenses have not

---

[11] "Ahead of PM Modi's visit, top US Senators voice concern over religious freedom in India," *The Indian Express*, May 25, 2016.

[12] *Ibid.*

[13] "No 'compassion' for NGO in India leaves Kerry worried," *The Hindu*, October 18, 2016.

[14] "The Kerry effect: Centre lifts curbs on fund transfers by NGO," *The Hindu*, updated December 1, 2016.

[15] See Foreign Contribution (Regulation) Act, 2010, Section 12 Subsection 4, https://fcraonline.nic.in/home/PDF_Doc/FC-RegulationAct-2010-C.pdf

[16] http://www.hindustantimes.com/india-news/fcra-registered-ngos-halved-in-two-years-10-000-more-ngos-lose-fcra-licence/story-vkVod2CLyjedTmpuYUoF6J.html

been renewed and another 1700 or so organizations whose renewal applications have been closed.[17] The vast majority of these organizations are small local NGOs who were affiliates of larger organizations who themselves were the primary recipients of foreign funds and who then disbursed them to local affiliates. But there have been higher-profile organizations who have run afoul of FCRA.

Such high-profile cases include Mercy Corps, National Endowment for Democracy, and the George Soros' Open Society Foundations, all of which are currently on the "prior permission" list. Greenpeace, a prominent environmental NGO based in Washington, D.C. came under heavy scrutiny by the Indian government in 2014, which claimed that the NGO's activities, research, and peaceful protests were "working against the economic progress of the country."[18] Greenpeace's FCRA registration was then cancelled in August 2015 due to alleged failure to disclose the movement of funds properly.[19] This cancellation was seen by many observers as heralding a new phase in the interpretation of FCRA regulations wherein the Government of India altered the definition of activities considered harmful to the national interest.

The Ford Foundation has faced similar challenges. In March 2015, the foundation was placed in the "prior permission" category after the MHA reportedly found that it was funding non-FCRA registered NGOs, a violation of Section 7 of the FCRA. Earlier that year, the Gujarat government filed a complaint with the MHA that the Ford Foundation's funded "anti-India" activities of two NGOs–Sabrang Trust and Citizens for Justice and Peace, and requested that the FCRA registration of these two NGOs be cancelled.[20] After several months of seeking ministry clearance to process any foreign contributions, the Ford Foundation was taken off the government watch list and was granted the ability to fund its affiliates after registering under the Foreign Exchange Management Act (FEMA), which falls under the jurisdiction of the finance ministry and maintains even tighter regulations that that of FCRA.

These cases, including that of Compassion International, appear to follow a similar pattern. If the activities of an FCRA-registered NGO are perceived as contrary to government interests, these nonprofits are generally scrutinized and then moved to the "prior permission" list on charges of mismanagement of funds or failure to adhere to Article 7 of the FCRA.[21] It is important to stress that this is not unique to the current Indian government. Indeed the original FCRA regulations of 1976 were adopted during India's Emergency period when the government sought to restrict foreign funding for civil society organizations opposed to Mrs Gandhi's autocratic rule. Subsequent governments have seen benefit in maintaining the Act, and the 2010 revision under the previous United Progressive Alliance government was a more stringent version than before. Since May 2014,

---

[17] See https://fcraonline.nic.in/home/PDF_Doc/fcra_11319_03112016.pdf
[18] Itika Sharma Punit and Manu Balachandran, "How India Cracked down on Greenpeace," *Quartz*, September 4, 2015, http://qz.com/495212/timeline-how-india-cracked-down-on-greenpeace/
[19] Aneesha Mathur, "Centre cancels Greenpeace India's FCRA registration," *The Indian Express*, September 4, 2015, http://indianexpress.com/article/india/india-others/greenpeace-indias-fcra-registration-cancelled-govt/
[20] Express News Service, "MHA removes Ford Foundation from watch list," *The Indian Express*, March 20, 2016, http://indianexpress.com/article/india/india-news-india/mha-removes-ford-foundation-from-watch-list/
[21] Bharti Jain, "'Activities not conducive to national interest': Jaising NGO, 24 others denied FCRA licences," *Times of India*, November 12, 2016.

the National Democratic Alliance government has continued on a well-trod path of using FCRA to scrutinize NGOs. As in the past, this is an extremely worrying phenomenon, as it stifles civil society by clamping down on alternate viewpoints and hampering political, economic, ideological, and religious diversity, not to mention depriving innocent beneficiaries of much needed social services. In light of this trend, I endorse U.S. Ambassador to India Richard Verma's warning of the "potentially chilling effects" that these regulatory steps might have on NGOs and civil society in India.[22]

There is one other dimension to this issue, namely whether Christian faith-based NGOs like Compassion International are being singled out for scrutiny by the current government. Given the extremely large number of NGOs whose FCRA licenses have been canceled in the past year and a half (over 11,000 and counting), one is inclined to say that the 'crackdown' on NGOs receiving foreign funds is not just focused on Christian organizations. But anecdotal evidence suggests that a fuller investigation is warranted. The FCRA regulations allow the government to cancel the license of any NGO deemed to be engaging in religious conversions under clauses that deem activities that upset 'religious harmony' as against the national interest. Christian faith-based organizations have been under great scrutiny by supporters of the current Indian government on this dimension, and social activism by the right-wing against alleged coerced conversions is extremely high. Soon after the transition to the NDA government, there was a national *Ghar Wapsi* campaign in which marginalized communities were pressured to "convert" back to Hinduism by illiberal elements.[23] This follows a long and troubled record of attacks against Christian missionaries by Hindu extremists.[24] The decision in March 2016 to deny visas to the United States Commission on International Religious Freedom is especially worrisome in this context.[25]

To my knowledge, no systematic analysis of the denial of FCRA licenses has yet been conducted to ascertain whether Christian organizations are disproportionately at risk. But a superficial glance suggests some cause for concern. India's Ministry of Home Affairs provides lists of associations whose licenses have not been renewed. A glance at these lists[26] suggests that a large number of these are faith-based Christian organizations and those serving tribal and lower-caste communities in extremely impoverished areas of India. Even if one assumes no malign intent, and attributes the loss of license to the higher obstacles being placed in front of these associations, the normative consequences are great as the most depressed parts of Indian society, which are extremely reliant on charitable support, are now being cut off from this aid. And, if, in fact, many of these organizations have chosen not to renew their FCRA licenses for fear of undue government scrutiny into their activities, it would only underscore Amb. Verma's warning of a chilling effect on civil society in India.

---

[22] Nida Najar, "U.S. Ambassador criticizes India's crackdown on charities and activist groups," *New York Times*, May 6, 2015.

[23] For example, see Annie Gowen, "Christian enclave in India fears violence as Hindus press for conversions," *Washington Post*, December 18, 2014.

[24] See Raveena Aulakh, "Anti-Christian violence in India sparks fears," *Toronto Star*, March 19, 2015.

[25] See Suhasini Raj, "India denies visa request from religious freedom monitoring group," *New York Times*, March 4, 2016.

[26] See https://fcraonline.nic.in/home/PDF_Doc/FCRA_Cases_02112016.pdf and https://fcraonline.nic.in/home/PDF_Doc/fcra_11319_03112016.pdf (Accessed 05 December 2016).

## Conclusion

India is a vital partner for the United States in the 21st century. Both countries have invested significant political capital in building this relationship and the fruits of these efforts are now being reaped in the form of more meaningful defense agreements, cooperation on energy and environmental policy dialogues, and deepening commercial ties that bind the world's signal democracies to each other. Consolidating these gains requires conceptualizing the relationship as strategic rather than transactional. Even strong partners can and will disagree on policies, and such disagreements cannot be allowed to derail the burgeoning collaboration. Yet a sure indicator of the strength of the bond is whether it can withstand some pressure. Given U.S. values and commitments to principles of religious freedom, the United States should respond to the trends documented above in a manner that continues to prioritize its strategic partnership with India, while also recognizing its own ability to use leverage against the country if it continues to engage in practices that are harmful to civil society. India's positive decision to reconsider its position on Ford Foundation's status was arguably in response to spotlights shone on its practices by Congress, Secretary Kerry, and Amb. Verma.[27] This indicates a susceptibility to pressure that can be leveraged to demand more transparent applications of FCRA rules and stronger commitments to protecting religious minorities in India even if the government appears reluctant thus far to do the same for Compassion International.[28]

---

[27] Bharti Jain, "Ford Foundation said to be off 'prior permission' list," *The Times of India*, January 8, 2016.
[28] Bharti Jain, "Government has no immediate plans to lift curbs on US-based NGO Compassion International," *Times of India*, October 18, 2016.

Chairman ROYCE. Thank you, Dr. Nooruddin.

I am going to go now to Mr. Eliot Engel of New York.

Mr. ENGEL. Dr. Nooruddin, I just have one quick question. Mr. Oakley and Mr. Sifton were talking about Compassion International, and I wondered—the experience that Compassion International is going through—are other NGOs facing this kind of harassment in the magnitude that Compassion International seems to be hassled?

And what should, in your opinion—we have a new administration coming in—what should that administration say to the Indian Government, knowing full well that our relationship with India is a very important and strategic relationship, getting warmer, getting better. We all like it. We all think it is important, and we think the Indian diaspora here in the United States plays a major role.

You know, it is sort of a delicate diplomatic move where you want to whisper in your friend's ear, and you want to tell them that you are not happy with certain things, but you don't want to worsen the relationship. You don't want to ruin it. How do we create that delicate balance? What should we be doing there?

Mr. NOORUDDIN. Thank you for a very good question. Let me start with the first one, which is in some sense easier even if it is not a very positive answer. Is Compassion International alone in its experience, the short answer is no. As I said, over 11,500 NGOs have not had their licenses renewed over the last couple of years. Now, to be fair, a lot of these are affiliates of foreign-backed NGOs. So the FCRA regulations require that any money that is dispersed through an association by, say, Compassion International, the recipients of that money have to also have FCRA licenses. So there are a lot of associations.

High-profile examples that have already been mentioned are Greenpeace, but others include the National Endowment for Democracy and the Ford Foundation, both of which ran afoul of FCRA regulators, lost their licenses, and only after some negotiations has the Ford Foundation, for instance, been reinstated though under a completely different instrument of the Indian Government that is arguably just as stringent and intrusive in managing how the Ford Foundation will function.

So I don't think this is just about Compassion International. I think it is very widespread and quite broad.

The broader question of, you know, how do we do this in a way that recognizes that this is an important relationship, that these are very centrally sensitive domestic politics questions in India, the core issue, I think, in a lot of this discussion is that the Indian Government is deeply concerned and has been across governments, but maybe more so today, about religious harmony, or put differently, the risk of communal discord at the local level.

This communal discord occurs when local actors complain that a local association is using its NGO status to proselytize, to evangelize, to convert people to Christianity, even if that is not, in fact, what they are doing. This, then, you know, percolates up to Delhi where the Ministry of Home Affairs will then choose to investigate.

So I think the Indian Government is increasing it because of its own definition of antinational activities is likely to put a real damper on many of these sorts of things. And, yet, the diplomatic relationship is very deep. There was a great deal of concern in India that we will return to a transactional relationship between India and the United States as opposed to a strategic relationship. This is meant to suggest that what India won't respond well to is being told, if you don't do this, here is what we are going to pull away. Right? They want to see a strong, deep relationship that can survive temporary disagreements. But I think on our end, that requires that we take them at their word for it and be willing to ask very hard questions about this.

You mention the diaspora population. So let me say in closing, the diaspora population in the United States is an extremely generous, charitable population which gives back to India lots of money benefiting education and social services.

All of that money is also at risk if the FCRA is used to go after charitable organizations that the Indian Government sees as being unpleasant.

American businesses doing work in India are going to be held under corporate social responsibility requirements. All of those contributions are going to be at risk if suddenly the Indian Government can scrutinize how those moneys are given. So this is not just about a particular NGO and a particular agenda. This really becomes a relationship of all American citizens who want to contribute to India's development suddenly worrying about whether their money is going to be impounded, whether their partners in India are going to be scrutinized and at the risk of criminal offenses.

So I think we have a great diplomat—I applaud Ambassador Verma for the work he has done while he has been in office. I think he should be empowered by you to come here to speak frankly to a good friend in India and hopefully the conversation will improve rather than worsen.

Chairman ROYCE. Thank you. Well, thank you, Dr. Nooruddin.

I would follow up maybe also with just a thought. Besides communicating with our Ambassador, and of course, we have communicated with the former Ambassador of India here, do you have any other thoughts about how we can dialogue on this issue? Of particular concern to me is what is going to happen, you know, if we end up without the ability to have Americans support these 145,000 Indian families that sort of rely on it in terms of whether the children are going to get an education or enough food?

Mr. NOORUDDIN. Chairman Royce, I think that is a fair question. I wish I had an optimistic answer to give. As you point out, bureaucracy is a stubborn thing. And it is—the Ministry of Home Affairs, which is, I will give you, the most powerful of India's ministries, has taken a very strong position on this in ways that are going to make it politically difficult for them to back down in any way that suggests they are backing down to external pressure.

There is a strong domestic constituency in India, however, that is deeply concerned about Christian missionaries' activities that frankly forms the support base for the current government. And so I think they are going to want to pay attention to that.

Chairman ROYCE. But, doctor, here is the point, and this is a conversation I had with the Ambassador: We are fairly familiar with the operations of Compassion, because they also operate in Indonesia, a country that likewise, would be concerned about conversions in activity. And what we have found is that largely, this is a myth. They are not involved proactively in doing that. It is a rumor. And so the suggestion, which I think is an easy one, to resolve the issue, is that if you have a particular channel partner—you know, there are 580 channel partners that are involved in that, all right, you take that off the table, but you allow the rest of the families here in the United States to write those checks to continue to support that effort and to not only give moral support but give the opportunity for those younger kids in these families, in situations that are so challenged, where they can actually complete their education. I mean, it just seems to me that there are the makings here for a compromise in this, which keeps the program open.

And maybe I could ask Mr. Oakley on that question. Going forward, is there an opportunity to move forward in a way that would guarantee the support for the destitute that rely on the contributions that come into the country?

Mr. OAKLEY. Thank you, Mr. Chairman. Currently, no, there is no path that we see as long as the current MHA order, the prior clearance order, which you all have a copy of, is in place. That order prevents Compassion's funds from being credited to the recipients without the prior approval of the Ministry of Home Affairs. We have worked for 7 months to obtain that prior approval, and we have been unsuccessful.

Chairman ROYCE. So let us say for a minute, though, that there was a change of heart, and a decision to go channel partner by channel partner, you have 580 channel partners, and to just review the channel partners and those that are not engaged in activities of—I mean, it seems rather dogmatic to shut down the largest program, whole scale, that offers financial support to this sector in India.

Mr. OAKLEY. Thank you. We completely agree. And, of course, we have submitted over 120 channel partners for review by the Ministry of Home Affairs. To this point, they have not even responded to our requests for that prior clearance for that group.

And in point of fact, some months ago, when we first heard that there were a few—they describe it as a few black sheep in the flock. We said, tell us who those black sheep are, and we will within 24 hours separate our partnership with them to alleviate all of your concerns. So that was our offer to them.

Subsequently, we agreed to not partner with any channel partner that had not received its NGO before the deadline—excuse me—its FCRA before the deadline to receive it, and that too did not produce any desired results. Our inability to communicate with MHA directly has been a source of significant frustration.

Chairman ROYCE. So there is the outline, obviously, for a resolution that would fit within their perspective if the decision could be made to look individually at these channel partners and then release the funds.

Well, let me—my time has expired. Let me go to Mr. Bera next.

Mr. BERA. Thank you, Mr. Chairman.

When I think about where we are in the U.S.-India relationship in a broad scope, it is at, really, a peak right now in terms of bilateral trade, in terms of bilateral security cooperation, in terms of—you know, if you look at where the diaspora is, here in the United States as well, it is also hitting a high note.

I am the only Indian-American Member of Congress currently, and I am thrilled that I will be joined in the House of Representatives by three additional members in the 115th Congress and our first Indian-American Senator. So in that, the diaspora is starting to step up, and as Dr. Nooruddin mentioned, is extremely philanthropic. And I would venture most of that philanthropy is going back to India.

And my concern with how this issue is resolved is that we don't want to decrease that philanthropy. We don't want to discourage folks, not just the diaspora but others that want to do good around the world from continuing to contribute and make those donations.

And in my conversations with the chairman, that is my concern. If you have one ministry, if you have someone in the MHA setting policy, that potentially becomes disruptive to many other NGOs, that is just a bad precedent. I understand the sensitivities in India as well, that they don't want to see the House of Representatives or a foreign government dictating what their own domestic policy should be. But from my perspective and my review, Compassion International has done everything that they can to be transparent to meet the guidelines and the compliance here and continue to do the work that they do along with other NGOs.

I would be curious, in terms of just following up on the ranking member's question, Dr. Nooruddin, the role that the diaspora might be able to play here in terms of resolving some of these issues, again, understanding that the diaspora increasingly is making philanthropic investments in India.

Mr. NOORUDDIN. The diaspora, I think, especially with four Indian-Americans in Congress, a first Indian-American Senator and possibly an Indian-American as the U.S. Representative to the United Nations, is a source of great pride in India. Many newspapers reported the day after the election about your success and your colleagues' success as much as they reported on the result of the Presidential election. I mean, it is a tremendous source of pride.

So I think that this is, in fact, a great point of leverage. There is a population in the United States that is very deeply engaged at home in India through their philanthropy. Their philanthropy goes through exactly the kind of work that Compassion International does in serving those that are most marginalized, especially children. And so I think the Indian-American community can understand that its voice will be heard in India, that it should recognize that if it signals to the Indian Government that an attack on Compassion International or any of these other NGOs that are doing the work that are trying to abide by the rules is going to be perceived as an attack on their own work, that they see that their contributions are likely to be addressed. Because I think this is will be heard loud and clear.

This is not a relationship, meaning with the diaspora population, that the Indian Government wants to endanger. They do see this as a real strategic strength and also as one that has, you know, crossed domain and that it brings commercial ties and all sorts of other things back.

I also think that, you know, the issue that you kind of hinted at in your remarks, Mr. Bera, concern about the definition of antinational. One of my colleagues on the panel also remarked about this, but really the most worrisome part of the FCRA regulations has been that the Indian Government has adopted a very wide interpretation of what constitutes antinational activity.

In the case of Greenpeace the cited reason was that in highlighting the potential environmental damage of some industrial projects, Greenpeace would hurt India's economy and this is, therefore, antinational. If that is the—if talking about Christianity to young children might induce some of them to be attracted to convert thereby upsetting other actors in the village, and that this is, then, deemed antinational, in effect, what antinational becomes is a license that anything the government doesn't agree with is antinational.

So there is no end in sight for that. And I think all of us who want to see India develop, who want to contribute to the most impoverished have a reason to want to have a much more transparent interpretation of that ruling and one that is consistent with principles of freedom of speech and association and of religious freedom.

Mr. BERA. Thank you.

Chairman ROYCE. Mr. Smith.

Mr. SMITH. Thank you, Chairman Royce.

First of all, to Mr. Oakley, thank you and Compassion for your extraordinary work living out Matthew 25, clothing the naked, feeding the hungry. I, like many members of this committee, are great admirers of your work, and I want to thank you for that worldwide, including in India.

Let me just ask a question with regards to the threat to Compassion International, and I think many of you have already suggested this, is really the bitter fruit of a multi-year, ever-escalating attack on NGOs. It is happening in India. The International Religious Freedom Report in 2016 notes that in April 2015, the Ministry of Home Affairs revoked the licences of nearly 9,000 charitable organizations, and it points out that it really is because of their poor record, pointing out the poor record of India on human trafficking, labor conditions, religious freedom, environmental food issues as well, and I would add child abduction where they have scored horrifically with the most recent report under the Goldman Act. So there are a myriad of issues. And like China, India is just defaulting to throw them out.

Later I am chairing the hearing as chairman of the Congressional-Executive Commission on China, on a look back over the last 8 years. We have seven people, all of whom have spent time in the Gulag, the lao gai as they call it in China, for their faith and for human rights causes. And we have had an inferior, weak, feckless response to China when it has come to human rights. And the parallels, particularly on the NGO laws, especially on the religious faith issue, it takes a turn in the curve, if you will, or a bend in the curve or the path, because in China it is to get to atheism.

In India, it is to get to Hinduism rather than allowing, as the Constitution of India prescribes, a true robust religious freedom. It is being usurped by the current regime, but it does go back some years ago.

In 2014, Hindu nationalists announced a reconvert effort. So, again, the bitter fruit of that is being realized. And, of course, six Indian states have very, very strong anti-conversion laws.

And, again, the U.S. Commission on Religious Freedom points out, and this is 2015, religious intolerance deteriorated, religious freedom violations increased, and they point out it is on a poor trajectory.

It seems to me that the United States has a moral duty, our Government, to put a tourniquet to the greatest extent possible on this deterioration. And I would ask you, if you would, maybe Mr. Sifton, you might want to speak to this, because you did say the U.S. Government needs to respond. Has it, and has it done so in a way that is likely to achieve the results? By CPC designation under the International Religious Freedom Act it seems to me, perhaps the time has come now to so designate India.

It does work in some countries to say, look, we are not kidding. You can't do this to Compassion. You can't do this to all of these other faiths including Muslims, and we are just going to turn the blind eye.

Secondly, do you see a parallel, Mr. Sifton, especially, with China? It seems like the NGOs become the enemy if they don't comport to the government policies, and to what they conceive or believe is the way forward. India is a democracy, unlike China. We would expect far more from India than we are getting.

So if you can speak to those issues, CPC designation and the parallels to China.

Mr. SIFTON. Well, there is no doubt. There is no doubt at all. There is worldwide crackdown on civil society underway, and this is but one example. Hindu nationalism in India is at the heart of what is going on in India.

CPC designation, generally, needs to be overhauled. I have great respect for the current Ambassador, but the fact of the matter is when countries like Vietnam and India are not on the list, it creates huge questions about the criteria that are being used.

I think the U.S. Government has a way in that is diplomatic and polite, the way two democracies can speak to each other effectively. The two principles I would recommend to the incoming administration and to this Congress is, A, parity. An Indian tycoon can give money to an American NGO like ACLU or pro-life group or pro-choice group, no questions asked. As long as it meets tax codes, it is fine. There are foreign agent laws, but that is for lobbying.

The fact of the matter is an Indian NGO can give $1 million to an American organization. I, if I were a millionaire, which I am not, I cannot so freely give money to the Lawyers, Collective or Compassion. That is a question of parity.

The second is consistency through the foreign investment vein of this current government. The Modi government is asking for foreign contributions. It is asking for international money to flow into the country from investment and, yet, when it comes to this type of money, the door closes.

And I would just say—I mean, you can say this politely, but what is the biggest threat to the entity of India? Compassion's work, the Lawyers Collective's work, or Kentucky Fried Chicken? I don't know. I mean, I think it is a question of consistency. You say to them, if you are going to do this, you have to do it consistently, and we have to have parity. U.S. and India are allies, democracies, and we have to have the same approach to be——

Mr. SMITH. Would you recommend CPC designation now? Because it can be done at any time. Normally, it is done on a designated—yes.

Mr. SIFTON. I would think that the incoming Ambassador should give it a very hard look.

Chairman ROYCE. Congresswoman Karen Bass from Los Angeles.

Ms. BASS. Thank you, Mr. Chair.

And let me thank the witnesses for your testimony today.

And also, I don't know if it was staff or who put this information together, but I was happy to learn that there were several hundred sponsors in my district for Compassion's work. I have a large Indian population, and it is nice to know that they are actively involved in Compassion.

I really wanted to continue along the responses from Mr. Sifton in terms of what is really behind this. And I understand that the FCRA was established to keep foreign money out of politics, but it seems like you are saying it was far more than that. I was wondering if you could provide a little more of the historical context, what was going on that led to it. And then I would also like to know more about Compassion's work.

Mr. SIFTON. I will just say really quickly, the testimony of my copanelists about the origins of law is correct, it was primarily a political control issue, similar to the legislation that Senator Fulbright moved through in the 1960s on the foreign agents law.

The great irony, though, is just this year there were amendments to the FCRA that loosened the regulations for giving to political parties, which is an amazing irony to this whole thing and the history of it. But perhaps my copanelists would like to talk more about it.

Mr. NOORUDDIN. Just on the background of the FCRA, I mean, and as I remarked and as Mr. Sifton just corroborated, the roots of this were to keep money out of politics, but what that really meant was to keep money out of civil society that took positions on issues that might be deemed sensitive to politicians.

Ms. BASS. So was there a specific case that was happening in India? I understand what you just said.

Mr. NOORUDDIN. Right.

Ms. BASS. But in terms of the catalyst for it.

Mr. NOORUDDIN. No, ma'am. The context was in 1976, during what in India we refer to as the Emergency period, in 1975 the then Prime Minister suspended civil liberties and established what was called the Emergency. It was in that period that this was passed, and the concern was that money could come into civil society actors that were pushing back against the Emergency legislation.

Ms. BASS. I see, thank you.

And then Compassion?

Mr. OAKLEY. Thank you, Congresswoman.

Briefly, in terms of the work that we do in India, across the world really, we believe in holistic child development. So we are interested in the physical, mental, emotional, and spiritual needs of the child to break the cycle of poverty.

I will tell you one of the things I find most interesting about this specific case with India, we push approximately $45 million a year in aid just to India, and by their own calculation the income tax commissioner of India has evaluated our operations at length and determined that merely 4 percent of that $45 million a year is for moral and spiritual values education. The remaining 96 percent, the overwhelming majority, is for all the types of humanitarian interventions you are used to seeing—provision of nutrition, food, clothing, medicine, school tuition, et cetera.

Ms. BASS. So it is my understanding you work with children that are designated as undesirable.

Mr. SIFTON. Correct. Our population, our criteria for entry into our program is that you are either a child in poverty, as defined by the World Bank, less than $1.90 per day, or extreme poverty of less than $1.25 per day. That is the only criteria. There is no condition based upon religion or any other category.

Ms. BASS. I see. Thank you.

I yield back my time.

Chairman ROYCE. We go to Congressman Matt Salmon from Arizona.

Mr. SALMON. Thank you.

I just have two questions and they are, I think, very similar in nature. Question number one is, does the Indian Government have the capacity to fill the void that has happened with these children, the services for these children? Do they even have the capacity to fill the void? And second, if they do, are they doing anything to try to fill that void?

Mr. OAKLEY. Thank you, Congressman Salmon.

The answer is no. Currently, the worldwide population of children in poverty is around 300 million, and, unfortunately, one-third of those, over 100 million of those are in India alone. So Compassion is actually just dealing with a very, very small fraction of that. The 145,000 children that are under our care, there will be no provision for them in the eventuality that we have to exit the country. They will become part of that 100 million who are either entirely underserved or underreached.

Mr. SALMON. My experience in dealing with humanitarian crises all over the world has been that the best deliverer of services, bar none, that I have seen anywhere on the globe are faith-based NGOs and faith-based initiatives. And I think it would be really tragic, really tragic, if we are not able to get the Indian Government to rethink this whole process in the name of the children. And I applaud you for your wonderful, wonderful work. And I think it is incumbent on us.

We do have a great relationship, bilateral relationship with India. But even when you have great relationships, even in marriage when you have a great relationship—I have been married 37 years, I have a great relationship, and my wife still tells me when I do things wrong. And I love her for it. It is a great thing. And

I think that even with a great partner like India we should be very, very outspoken about resuming the great work that you are doing and getting those children cared for.

So thank you very much.

Mr. OAKLEY. Thank you for that comment. And I would just like to reiterate that our desire is overwhelmingly to work with the Government of India to resolve this. We have been there for almost 50 years and we would love to be there for another 50. We believe that the diversity of India, religiously, ethnically, is a strength, not a weakness. They should lean into that. And we will help them as part of helping all of their poor kids.

Mr. SALMON. Thank you. Mr. Chairman, I yield back.

Chairman ROYCE. If the gentleman would yield.

I think have you about 3 weeks left before the decision to just have to vacate entirely the program in India?

Mr. OAKLEY. Correct, Mr. Chairman. We have simply run out of funds. We are unable to get funds into the country. We are actually faced with the problem that if we depart, we may not have funds to pay the legally obligated gratuity and severance benefits for our employees there. There are 6,000 people in India who are employed by Compassion funds through our channel partners. We have no provision for winding up in an orderly fashion if we can't work with the government.

Chairman ROYCE. Let me go to Jeff Duncan of South Carolina.

Mr. DUNCAN. Thank you, Mr. Chairman.

First off, I want to thank you for your unwavering support for what Compassion International is doing and your focus on the children in India. I was proud when Prime Minister Modi came and spoke to a joint session of Congress last year, and I want to use my time to call on him at this point and the Modi government to end the pre-approval requirement for Compassion so that money can flow to where the rubber meets the road and where the needs are most dire.

Mr. Oakley, how many children qualify as living in extreme poverty globally?

Mr. OAKLEY. Currently, extreme poverty would be 300 million, as I mentioned earlier. And about a one-third of that exists just in the nation of India and a fair bit in the South Asia area as well.

Mr. DUNCAN. Right. Does Compassion accept children of all faiths?

Mr. OAKLEY. Absolutely. There is no criteria of religion for admission to our program, simply economic need.

Mr. DUNCAN. So my understanding is Compassion really focuses on holistic child development programs. Is the spiritual component of Compassion's holistic approach contextualized in any way?

Mr. OAKLEY. Thank you. Absolutely. We operate in 26 countries, in all three areas of the world, Asia, Africa and Latin America. And we understand, we recognize very well that each of those is very different. We have to contextualize our programming, both for the region that we are in, and it has to be contextualized from an age perspective.

So to the extent that there is a spiritual and values-driven component to our programming, it is age appropriate, it is culturally appropriate. We teach values that transcend all of the world's great religions. The values that we are teaching in India would be values taught by the Hindu faith, by the Muslim faith, Buddhist faith. They would transcend each of those religions.

Mr. DUNCAN. So let me ask you this. If Compassion has to exit India, what are the implications for other faith-based NGOs there?

Mr. OAKLEY. This is the concern I mentioned at the outset that troubles me greatly, because so many NGOs that are operating in India are doing so on budgets that are much smaller than ours, they don't have the network that we have. Certainly access to this forum is not something that is available to them easily.

And if Compassion were to exit India, I really do feel that we sort of represent the canary in the coal mine, that if we go, the Indian Government has taken down the largest child sponsorship agency in the world, the largest importer of foreign NGO funds into India. They understand at that point there is very little to stop them from taking the same type of action against other NGOs.

And I appreciated the comments of my colleagues earlier that if anti-national activity is anything the government doesn't agree with, it is not just the faith-based NGO community, it is a number of civil society organizations that have expressed opinions or have policies and platforms that are in opposition to those of the government, or perhaps simply not as aligned as the government would prefer. That is not—I hope that is not anti-national activity in India.

So the trend here—I like to look at trends, where is it going—the trend is heading in the wrong direction. And this would be a significant bellwether to the Indian Government that their effort to stop NGOs that have positions with which they do not agree is working.

Now, the Government of India, we do not intend to tell them what to do or how to do what they do. They are a sovereign nation. But they are also signatories and have ratified the ICCPR, and those provisions, by signing and ratifying that document, they have agreed to allow the freedom of expression of religion, freedom of political speech, all of those freedoms.

So those are under attack and they fail to recognize that using policy in this fashion and using regulatory requirements and legal requirements in this fashion and then not following their own legal requirements in doing so, it is in violation of their own law and it is in violation of international law.

Mr. DUNCAN. I co-chair the Sovereignty Caucus here in Congress, and I fully respect the sovereignty of nations to do what is in their best interest and what they feel like they need to do, so I don't intend any of my comments to trample on the sovereignty of India. But this is an urging of the United States Congress to the Modi government to embrace an organization that is filling a void.

To piggyback on what Mr. Salmon said, the Indian Government doesn't have the capacity to help the children that Compassion and other NGOs help.

And so let me ask you this. Are there any other pre-approval requirements in any other countries that Compassion helps?

Mr. OAKLEY. No, we currently do not have a pre-approval requirement in any of our 26 countries. And I can tell you from personal experience, I have spent the last 3 years working on this case, this is our hardest country to work in from a political and regulatory perspective.

Mr. DUNCAN. I am about out of time. Let me just ask this final question. Has Compassion broken any laws in India?

Mr. OAKLEY. None.

Mr. DUNCAN. Wow. Okay.

Mr. Chairman, thank you for your work. I yield back.

Ms. ROS-LEHTINEN [presiding]. Thank you so much, sir.

And now we will turn to Mr. Chabot of Ohio.

Mr. CHABOT. Thank you, Madam Chairman.

Mr. Oakley, is there any there any action that the Indian Government could take to enable Compassion to continue its operations in India?

Mr. OAKLEY. Yes, there is. Thank you, Congressman. I believe the immediate step that would allow us to restore operations in the next 3 weeks would be rescinding the MHA's prior approval order of February 2016. That would allow funds to move directly from us to the 500-plus channel partners that are supporting the 145,000 children.

Secondarily, we have to be able to pay our field staff on the ground. We have two locally incorporated entities, one in Kolkata, one in Chennai. Presently, both of those charitable entities have had their FCRAs revoked, although they had been in place for more than a decade. If those were restored—because we think the revocation was in violation of law, certainly there was no notice, no indication as to why they were revoked—if those were restored, we could continue to pay our people who are assisting the children under our sponsorship.

Mr. CHABOT. Thank you. And if they would take that action, how many children would be affected and what would that effect be on their lives?

Mr. OAKLEY. So presently, we had 145,000 children under our care as of this summer. Because of our decision to unilaterally, as a gesture of good faith, drop our partnership with any channel partner that had not received its FCRA as of the end of September, we actually departed 15,000 children at that time. So the 130,000 that are remaining are still under our care, although the operations for many of them are suspended at this time.

If those operations could be restored quickly, the aid that we give, the food, the medicine—the school tuition is critically important because the school year is just about to commence in February in India and you have to enroll your kid and you have to pay tuition there, they have uniform requirements, all of these things— all of that could be restored quickly.

And our commitment to the Indian Government would be we will be as transparent, as open, as cooperative as we can with you. If you are concerned about any project and whether or not there is anti-national or conversion activity going on at that location, tell us. We will work with you. We will eliminate that partner for as long as you have a concern about that partner. That dialogue has been something that has an eluded us thus far.

Mr. CHABOT. So if the Indian Government would take the action that you have recommended and that is the number of children that would be affected, on, say, a typical day, what are the types of things that you all do and what impact on a daily basis would it have on these children's lives?

Mr. OAKLEY. Absolutely. In India that is a fairly high-touch country for us, U.S. dollars go a long way. That is a very efficient place for us to operate. So the contact time with a child is quite high. Our programs run 5 to 6 days a week. These are child development centers that are attached to the local Christian church. They will receive one to two meals a day there. They will receive medical treatment if they need it, evaluations as to their health. They will also receive tutoring that is age appropriate related to the studies that they are doing.

In some cases, we have medical interventions that are much higher need, surgeries, those types of things. Those will occur as well on a regular basis, particularly given the size of the population that we have in India. It is our largest country at present.

Mr. CHABOT. Thank you.

And then finally, if the Indian Government does not take this action that we have discussed here, is there some other organization that is ready to step in and aid those children in the ways that you have just described.

Mr. OAKLEY. That is a fantastic question. We have wrestled with that at length. As part of withdrawing, if we are forced to withdraw, we would very much desire to do so in an orderly fashion that is compliant with the law, as well as make provision for the transfer of some of those children to other NGOs operating in country, secular, faith based, just provide for them.

We have done some preliminary analysis on that point. We think we could transfer potentially 10,000 to 15,000 children, nowhere near the 130,000 that we currently care for. The primary problem is distance. You have to be able to travel by foot typically to a child development center to receive the services we provide. So we have to find an equivalent somewhere within foot distance, and that can be very hard.

Mr. CHABOT. So it would be safe to say that if the government doesn't take that action, there are some children that are going to inevitably fall through the cracks here.

Mr. OAKLEY. Not some. It will be more than 80 percent.

Mr. CHABOT. Thank you. I yield back my time.

Chairman ROYCE [presiding]. Randy Weber of Texas.

Mr. WEBER. Thank you, Mr. Chairman.

Mr. Sifton, you said earlier in your remarks you suggested parity, there needed to be some parity there, in talking about the fact that they wouldn't allow U.S. dollars to go to Indian NGOs. By parity, are you saying that we should not allow any Indian money to come in? Explain that.

Mr. SIFTON. Certainly not. I think that would violate U.S. law.

Mr. WEBER. Move your mic over in front of you. There you go. Thank you.

Mr. SIFTON. No, certainly not, it is not a threat, but rather an exhortation to the Indian Government that your wealthy or more fortunate citizens are entitled to give money to nonprofits and churches and educational institutions here in the United States, we should be allowed—our citizens should be allowed to give money to the same institutions in India.

Mr. WEBER. It is almost like a trade agreement, isn't it?

Mr. SIFTON. I mean, the great irony here is that Prime Minister Modi is making enormous efforts to attract foreign investment, bring foreign money into India, but not this kind of money.

Mr. WEBER. Yeah. All right. Thank you.

Mr. Oakley, you said earlier the ICCPR was ratified by India. What is that?

Mr. OAKLEY. Apologies for using the acronym. It is the International Covenant on Civil and Political Rights. India is a country that has ratified it. And those obligations, countries commit to those obligations understanding that they supersede their local law, that they are committing to those, that those commitments will then be embedded in their national law.

Mr. WEBER. When did they sign that?

Mr. OAKLEY. I do not have the date, Congressman.

Mr. WEBER. How many countries have signed it? Do you know?

Mr. OAKLEY. I believe the vast majority of the countries of the world. There are perhaps one or two that have either not ratified it or done so with reservations that have gutted it.

Mr. WEBER. Any teeth to that agreement? I mean, if they don't hold up their end of the bargain or live up to that agreement what happens?

Mr. OAKLEY. Well, functionally, and this is true with most of the international covenants, enforcement is difficult, at least at a legal level. Typically what happens is there is dialogue around it raising awareness of the violations. It is almost an approach of shaming a country into abiding by their international commitments.

The other approach, which we do not desire, is to litigate this issue, which would take more than a decade, and it would really be on behalf of the other NGOs who are remaining in India.

Mr. WEBER. In your opinion, would it be worthwhile to have a resolution expressing the sense of Congress that they think India has violated this and it is going to have a dire effect on their most unfortunate?

Mr. OAKLEY. I think a resolution like that would be incredibly helpful from our perspective. But we are not alone. I think this would be incredibly helpful from the perspective of my colleagues here today and the broader civil society community.

Mr. WEBER. Okay.

Dr. Nooruddin, you also made the comment that your colleagues said that this was "discrimination disguised behind taxation," but that you didn't necessarily agree with that. Did I mis-hear that?

Mr. NOORUDDIN. I think you did not. If I may expand. I think to demonstrate that this is discrimination would require a much more systematic analysis. Eleven and a half thousand NGOs have lost their licenses in the last year and a half. They are not all Christian faith based.

Mr. WEBER. So they are equal opportunity discriminators is what that means.

Mr. NOORUDDIN. Well, maybe from their perspective they are equal opportunity appliers of a regulation that is not very transparent and is not very clear as to how you fall afoul of it. I think it is quite clear, and you can glance in my written testimony, I provide a link to the Indian Government Web site which lists the NGOs that have lost their licenses.

Just anecdotally, I just glanced at page one. There are 22 listed on page one. Nine of them have very obviously Christian names to them, invoking the Virgin Mary and invoking particular saints, et cetera.

So my guess, Congressman, is that the particular application of this law across the 11,500 might quite possibly have a religious dimension to it, but it is not only that. It is very much environmental organizations, it is pro-democracy organizations.

And of course there are a lot of organizations, as I mentioned up front, that were likely in violation of the law. They hadn't filed income taxes for 3 consecutive years that are required of the law, money had been channeled to places who had not gotten FCRA approval, et cetera.

So there is a big bag of associations that have run afoul of this particular regulation, and I just wanted to suggest that we want to think of the whole picture.

Mr. WEBER. Thank you. I am out of time. I appreciate it.

Chairman ROYCE. Reid Ribble of Wisconsin.

Mr. RIBBLE. Thank you, Mr. Chairman.

Good morning.

Dr. Nooruddin, if a citizen in India donates money to a religious organization, is it tax deductible there? Or if a corporation does, is it tax deductible there?

Mr. NOORUDDIN. No, sir.

Mr. RIBBLE. It is not?

Mr. NOORUDDIN. No.

Mr. RIBBLE. Okay. Thank you for that clarification.

I want to go back to be Mr. Oakley. Each of us were given a map like this, I appreciate you providing, I am assuming you provide the data. I am one of these sponsors. And Compassion just does amazing work in Wisconsin and around the world. My son Jared is a Compassion artist, has been for 10 years, and has raised tens of thousands, if not hundreds of thousands of dollars for your work.

But I will guarantee you before this day is out I will either have someone tweet at me or put a Facebook posting who has seen this and they are going to ask this question. I would like you to give you the opportunity to answer it, because you are going to be better equipped to answer it. And this question is not based in cynicism, it is just going to be a question they are going to ask.

And they are going to ask me, if the Indian Government doesn't want you there, and given that the needs around the world are so great, why would you not just redirect the money to other needs, to the Bolivians or the Hondurans or the Ethiopians? Would you mind answering that question for those folks?

Mr. OAKLEY. Absolutely. Thank you for the question, and thanks for your support and your son's support as well.

There are several answers to the question. One is simply, as I mentioned earlier, the extraordinary need in India. It has more children living in poverty than any other single country on Earth. So it is a great place for us to work with the poorest of the poor.

We could exit and apply those funds elsewhere, and certainly those funds would be well utilized elsewhere. That is not our hope.

We have been in India for a very long time. We see that the people of India, the people that we work with, the parents, the people within the poorest communities that we operate in, they want us to stay in India. They are incredibly grateful for the services we provide.

And so I think Compassion, I am speaking for myself, but I believe for my organization as well, we go where the greatest need is. To the extent we can work in conditions of extreme poverty that is where you get the most bang for your buck in terms of outcomes. By working with children, you have a longer runway for those outcomes to be effective.

We have had independent, third-party, peer-reviewed analysis of our program which determines that it works. So by operating in a country like India, which has over 130 million Muslims, it has got more than 50 million Christians, it is a diverse country religiously, in terms of ethnicities, languages, this is an extraordinary opportunity to help change the face of India by raising up its poorest children.

Mr. RIBBLE. Thank you for that answer.

And, Chairman Royce, I want you to know I would be completely supportive of whatever action this committee wants to take in relationship to this issue. It would be unfortunate indeed for the children of India to suffer the moral hazard of this choice if it results in you redirecting that money elsewhere in the world. Now, those other children would be the beneficiaries for sure, but that doesn't alleviate the problem in India. And so thank you for your work there and thank you for the work of Compassion.

I yield back.

Mr. OAKLEY. Thank you, Congressman.

Chairman ROYCE. Mr. Dana Rohrabacher of California.

Mr. ROHRABACHER. First of all, I would like to thank the chairman for focusing our attention on this issue. Mr. Chairman, you could have focused on any number of issues, and let me just say it speaks highly of you and your values that we have focused on something that 130,000 kids are going to have an immediate impact on. So thank you very much, Mr. Chairman.

I am trying to understand the overall issue here as well as the specific issue and challenge that you are facing here in Compassion. Is this part of a bigger picture? Look, we are suffering in parts of world of radical Islam, okay, and in this part of world maybe is this a result of Hindu fanaticism?

Mr. OAKLEY. Thank you for the question, Congressman.

It is difficult for me to get into the mind of another individual, let alone a political party in a country. I can tell you that based upon the timing of our challenges, having operated successfully for 45 years, and then to have a series of incredibly rigorous challenges in a very compressed period of time, in the last 3 years, in multiple contexts, so across different divisions of the Indian Government, and then looking at our own operation and recognizing that nothing has changed, everything that we are doing is the same.

And then personally I have sat with six different law firms and multiple chartered accountants in India and asked this very question, are we legally compliant? Is there something that we are doing that in fact breaks the law? And to a person I have heard that, no, you are operating within the law. And again, as I mentioned in my opening comments, to the extent that the law is being broken, it is being broken by the Indian Government.

Now, motive is difficult to understand. I will tell you that we operate in 26 countries, so I get a fairly high-level view of what is happening around the world and I see the rise of nationalism as being particularly concerning. It is very concerning in the Indian context, in part because of the numbers of minority groups that I mentioned earlier.

And my view, and I believe the view of our organization, is that a test of a democracy is how it treats its poorest, its most vulnerable, its smallest minorities, not whether or not it is pandering to the desires of the majority.

So from my perspective, I think something has changed in the last 3 years and the trend is going in the wrong direction.

Mr. ROHRABACHER. There are repercussions on these type of changes that we are talking about in the world, whether it is not just Hindu nationalism, not just radical Islam, but as you are expressed it today, you might say an upsurge of nationalism.

I would have to say I disagree with you as to whether or not that is something that is inherently going to take people in the wrong direction. Quite frankly, nationalism in the United States, for example, has I think really accomplished some great things, and that is overcoming local prejudices and local challenges where we face that we are a country of everybody, of so many different type of people that it is the nationalism that keeps us together as a country.

But with that said, I could see that some NGOs might actually, if they come in conflict with that spirit of nationalism, could basically end up in a conflict in that society where there were not conflicts before, which doesn't seem evident in your case.

But, for example, if you have NGOs that are focused on government policy rather than providing charitable givings to people in need, that would be, I could understand, where a newly nationalistic government would not want someone from the outside coming in and being financed, asking them for a change in their law. However, obviously the change in law that did happen in your case has resulted in 130,000 kids being put in jeopardy.

Let me again echo what my colleague just said in that whatever action this chairman would like to take on this to help you and your efforts to keep this charitable activity going in India, you will have our support and my support.

However, I do think that it is time, Mr. Chairman, for us also to put into perspective as we see nationalism rising around the world what NGOs are supposed to be about and what some NGOs—I mean, if we are talking about a country that has 30,000, did you say, NGOs?

Mr. OAKLEY. No, more like a million.

Mr. ROHRABACHER. A million NGOs. Something is wrong there. Maybe many of those NGOs could be classified here as political organizations. And I know that in several other countries that is what we have. I will have to just say in one country that I asked—well, I asked about the political prisoners in Russia. I asked for a list of all the political prisoners. For years I could not get that list, because everyone wants to portray Russia as having thousands of political prisoners.

Well, I got the list and there were a couple hundred people on the list, but a large percentage of them were on the list because they were part of Greenpeace. But they were not just part of Greenpeace, they were part of groups of people who went onto drilling platforms in the Arctic to try to prevent Russia from having Arctic drilling.

Now, sorry, that would be illegal in our country as well. That is not what an NGO should be all about, is forcing a policy on someone, as compared to even advocating it.

So I think that we need to have a closer look at NGOs, but I think your testimony today and this issue that we are talking about today really is valuable to us, because to understand that with—don't let us focus on some of these NGOs that are engaged with policy versus NGOs that are engaged with charity and how we must step forward. If we are going to save 130,000 kids, we need to get behind you. And that is a really important message for this hearing.

And thank you again, Mr. Chairman, for taking us here.

Chairman ROYCE. Thank you.

And on behalf of the committee, I want to recognize the outstanding work of Mr. Ribble of Wisconsin, who will, unfortunately, be retiring from the committee, as he is retiring from Congress. And I wanted to share with everybody how much I enjoyed working with him during his time here.

We traveled together to the Congo. He has a passion for children and children abroad. He has personal experience with adoption. And he used that to good effect to help us bring some ultimately 400 children who had been adopted to get them out of the Congo where they had been stuck.

He cares deeply about our Nation and its security. But also there is this private side of him that you saw a little bit about today, which is the fact that he is one of these donors. He and his family and his son donate to Compassion in order to reach a family abroad, in order to do what Amy Porter, my chief of staff, and her daughter do, which is to reach out to children in India and to provide them the means, the help, so that they can get an education and so that they might have enough food to eat.

I want to thank the witnesses also for their participation and the committee members. I think we have a better understanding of the issue. As we heard today, Compassion is helping Indian children who are living often on less than a dollar a day. And they are in desperate need and we are all very worried that their support, support coming from our constituents, several thousand constituents, for example, in my district, will end in a matter of 3 weeks if we do not figure out a resolution to this, and that would be a tragedy.

I mentioned the bureaucracy in my opening statement. It is the committee's sincere hope that this problem can be resolved in a way that allows for humane generosity to continue. The two great countries have so much in common. So many bridges have been built over the last 15 years. The ranking member, Eliot Engel, and I have been involved so much in this bridge building. And on top of it, we have the vision from the Prime Minister who leads India and his background as well.

So I think I can speak for the committee in asking that those in India involved in this decision focus on this immediate resolution so that we can then go on to focus on all the other issues that bring our two great democracies together.

Thank you very much. And with that, we are adjourned.

[Whereupon, at 11:40 a.m., the committee was adjourned.]

# APPENDIX

---

## MATERIAL SUBMITTED FOR THE RECORD

# FULL COMMITTEE HEARING NOTICE
## COMMITTEE ON FOREIGN AFFAIRS
U.S. HOUSE OF REPRESENTATIVES
WASHINGTON, DC 20515-6128

**Edward R. Royce (R-CA), Chairman**

December 6, 2016

## TO: MEMBERS OF THE COMMITTEE ON FOREIGN AFFAIRS

You are respectfully requested to attend an OPEN hearing of the Committee on Foreign Affairs, to be held in Room 2172 of the Rayburn House Office Building (and available live on the Committee website at http://www.ForeignAffairs.house.gov):

**DATE:**      Tuesday, December 6, 2016

**TIME:**      10:00 a.m.

**SUBJECT:**   American Compassion in India: Government Obstacles

**WITNESSES:**   Mr. Stephen Oakley
General Counsel and Vice President of the General Counsel Office
Compassion International

Mr. John Sifton
Acting Deputy Washington Director
Asia Advocacy Director
Human Rights Watch

Irfan Nooruddin, Ph.D.
Hamad bin Khalifa Professor of Indian Politics
Walsh School of Foreign Service
Georgetown University

### By Direction of the Chairman

*The Committee on Foreign Affairs seeks to make its facilities accessible to persons with disabilities. If you are in need of special accommodations, please call 202/225-5021 at least four business days in advance of the event, whenever practicable. Questions with regard to special accommodations in general (including availability of Committee materials in alternative formats and assistive listening devices) may be directed to the Committee.*

# COMMITTEE ON FOREIGN AFFAIRS
MINUTES OF FULL COMMITTEE HEARING

Day___*Tuesday*___Date_____*12/6/2016*_____Room_____*2172*_____

Starting Time _____*10:09*_____ Ending Time _____*11:38*_____

Recesses | *0* | (____ to ____) (____ to ____) (____ to ____) (____ to ____) (____ to ____) (____ to ____)

**Presiding Member(s)**
*Chairman Edward R. Royce, Rep. Ileana Ros-Lehtinen*

*Check all of the following that apply:*

Open Session ☑       Electronically Recorded (taped) ☑
Executive (closed) Session ☐   Stenographic Record ☑
Televised ☑

**TITLE OF HEARING:**

*American Compassion in India: Government Obstacles*

**COMMITTEE MEMBERS PRESENT:**

*See attached.*

**NON-COMMITTEE MEMBERS PRESENT:**

*none*

**HEARING WITNESSES: Same as meeting notice attached? Yes ☑ No ☐**
*(If "no", please list below and include title, agency, department, or organization.)*

**STATEMENTS FOR THE RECORD:** *(List any statements submitted for the record.)*

*SFR - Rep. Gerald Connolly*

TIME SCHEDULED TO RECONVENE _____
or
TIME ADJOURNED *11:38* _____

_____
Full Committee Hearing Coordinator

# HOUSE COMMITTEE ON FOREIGN AFFAIRS
*FULL COMMITTEE HEARING*

| PRESENT | MEMBER | | PRESENT | MEMBER |
|---|---|---|---|---|
| X | Edward R. Royce, CA | | X | Eliot L. Engel, NY |
| X | Christopher H. Smith, NJ | | | Brad Sherman, CA |
| X | Ileana Ros-Lehtinen, FL | | | Gregory W. Meeks, NY |
| X | Dana Rohrabacher, CA | | | Albio Sires, NJ |
| X | Steve Chabot, OH | | X | Gerald E. Connolly, VA |
| X | Joe Wilson, SC | | | Theodore E. Deutch, FL |
| | Michael T. McCaul, TX | | | Brian Higgins, NY |
| | Ted Poe, TX | | X | Karen Bass, CA |
| X | Matt Salmon, AZ | | | William Keating, MA |
| | Darrell Issa, CA | | X | David Cicilline, RI |
| | Tom Marino, PA | | | Alan Grayson, FL |
| X | Jeff Duncan, SC | | X | Ami Bera, CA |
| | Mo Brooks, AL | | X | Alan S. Lowenthal, CA |
| | Paul Cook, CA | | | Grace Meng, NY |
| X | Randy Weber, TX | | | Lois Frankel, FL |
| X | Scott Perry, PA | | X | Tulsi Gabbard, HI |
| X | Ron DeSantis, FL | | | Joaquin Castro, TX |
| | Mark Meadows, NC | | X | Robin Kelly, IL |
| X | Ted Yoho, FL | | | Brendan Boyle, PA |
| | Curt Clawson, FL | | | |
| | Scott DesJarlais, TN | | | |
| X | Reid Ribble, WI | | | |
| | Dave Trott, MI | | | |
| X | Lee Zeldin, NY | | | |
| X | Dan Donovan, NY | | | |

**Statement for the Record**
*Submitted by Mr. Connolly of Virginia*

The U.S.-India relationship is immensely consequential for U.S. foreign policy in the 21$^{st}$ century. Despite being a relationship colored by the Cold War tensions of the 20$^{th}$ century, it offers the United States the opportunity to promote broad-based prosperity, deepen commercial ties, and enhance security cooperation with a democracy of 1.25 billion people in the Asia-Pacific – a region the Obama Administration has prioritized for U.S. engagement abroad.

On August 30, 2016, the U.S. and India collaborated on two significant milestones that illustrate our enhanced strategic cooperation. U.S. Defense Secretary Ashton Carter and Indian Defense Minister Manohar Parrikar signed a landmark defense agreement, the Logistics Exchange Memorandum of Agreement, which facilitates exchange of logistics support, supplies, and services. On the same day, U.S. Secretary of State John Kerry and U.S. Secretary of Commerce Penny Pritzker co-chaired the second U.S.-India Strategic and Commercial Dialogue (S&CD) in New Delhi, India. I was glad to write Secretaries Kerry and Pritzker in support of this dialogue and addressing trade barriers to deepen our commercial relationship. The United States has become one of the largest defense-equipment suppliers to India, with contracts worth almost $13 billion over the last fifteen years. Beyond defense, U.S.-India trade relations are at an all-time high, with total trade volume exceeding $100 billion.

The U.S. and India have also collaborated on efforts to combat climate change. India currently produces about 4.5 percent of the world's greenhouse gas emissions, and seven of the ten most polluted cities in the world are in India. That is why it is notable that India formally ratified the Paris climate change agreement on October 2.

As with any close, bilateral relationship, we do have some areas of disagreement, including on space for civil society. Critical to any democratic society is the ability of its people to freely express ideas without fear of discrimination based on their ideology or creed.

India's Foreign Contributions Regulations Act (FCRA) regulates grants from foreign donors, and has reportedly been used to harass organizations that questioned or criticized government policies. The Indian Government claims that an American evangelical non-governmental organization (NGO), Compassion International, violated the FCRA by using some money claimed as charitable for non-charitable purposes. The Indian Government now requires the Ministry of Home Affairs to clear all of Compassion's foreign wire contributions, which has restricted the transfer of funds to many of the NGO's local partners. Compassion may now have to shut down its India operations due to lack of necessary funding for its activities.

The application of the FCRA law to restrict non-governmental activities is not unique to Compassion International. The Indian Ministry of Home Affairs, which grants foreign funding licenses under FCRA, has denied permission to many NGOs without explicit rationale other than that their activities are not in the "national interest." This justification has been a problem for some religiously affiliated organizations like Compassion, but also for political, social justice, and human rights organizations. As of November 2016, nearly 27,000 NGOs have been barred from receiving foreign funds since 2012, due to problems with their FCRA registration applications or other vague justifications. According to the Delhi-based *Hindustan Times*, this update marks a more than 50 percent decrease in the number of registered NGOs permitted to receive foreign funds in only two years.

The U.S.-India relationship is grounded in a sense of shared values, including mutual respect for human rights and religious freedom. Protection of these rights is an essential component of a stable and prosperous democratic society.

While the Full Committee's decision to hold a hearing related to U.S.-India relations for the first time in four years is welcome, we should expand the scope of our future work on this vital bilateral relationship to include the many significant policy dialogues taking place between our two democracies. As a strategic ally and indispensable partner of the United States, India holds enormous importance and potential. I look forward to a discussion of how U.S.-India ties continue to evolve and how Congress can play an active supporting role in the further cultivation of this pivotal relationship.

www.ingramcontent.com/pod-product-compliance
Lightning Source LLC
Chambersburg PA
CBHW081420280526
45788CB00009B/3180